# NECESSITY

## OF

# FINANCE

*An Overview of the Science of Management of Wealth
for an Individual, a Group, or an Organization*

## DR. ANTHONY M. CRINITI IV

CRINITI PUBLISHING

I would like to dedicate this book to my parents to whom I owe my life. They have made countless sacrifices for me so that I can one day fulfill my own dreams. I may never truly feel the pain of what you have been through to persistently guide such a difficult child and I may never be able to repay you. Instead, my educational accomplishments and this book was my plan to show you my appreciation.

# TABLE OF CONTENTS

# Preface

This book was created to assist many people in understanding the basics of finance, the science of wealth management for an individual, a group, or an organization. As a finance professor and former financial consultant, I have often witnessed the difficulties people have faced in understanding this very complex subject. Although many aspects of finance have very simple origins, the subject has evolved into the extremely complicated form we know today, particularly in the last fifty years. Many people complain that finance is too confusing. An individual's experience with finance may be better if he or she reads a preliminary book written in everyday terms that can help him or her to understand the subject more clearly before he or she engages in formal study. This book is a reflection of my attempt to demonstrate the complex nature of finance in a more understandable way.

The title of this text reflects a radical view of thinking about the subject of finance, which has simple roots in the beginning of civilization. However, modern finance, as taught in American universities, only began in the 1950s. Although it is taught as a separate subject, and the distinction between finance and economics and other similar subjects may seem obvious, many of the founding fathers of modern finance are self-admitted economists. Also most of the major theories were created by economists, physicists, mathematicians, etc. No wonder finance is often confused with other subjects.

With world wealth accumulating to its highest point in history, the necessity to understand this subject is more crucial than ever. This book highlights the need to give full respect to finance as a separate science and clears up many of the confusions with related subjects such as economics. It also coins the word "financialists" to identify the scientists in this field.

This book starts with an introduction about the need for finance. Next the definition, purpose, goals, and history of finance and economics are analyzed. This book also explores the basic terminology necessary to understanding finance. For example, what is the difference between money and wealth? What is the difference between investing and saving? What is risk and return? What is the time value of money? Other major financial questions are analyzed as well. For example, what are the different techniques for selecting investments? What are the different branches of finance that currently exist? What kinds of investments exist? What role does ethics play in finance?

Although this book is targeted at beginner to intermediate-level financial students and anyone interested in the subject with or without limited financial experience, it is also relevant for master-level students and beyond. For advanced students and practitioners, this book may serve as a tool to help reflect on and reevaluate the concepts they were taught in finance from a simpler alternative perspective. I believe simplicity, when demonstrated in its purest sense, has a way of transforming a concept or subject into something with a totally different meaning. I hope to have this effect. All I ask is that the advanced students and practitioners read this book with an open mind and deeply reflect on all of the simpler terms we often take for granted.

Finance is a very promising science that can be helpful to all who spend time studying and practicing it. However, I want to be clear that it is not easy for the average student. This book is not a substitute for your required college or university financial textbooks and reading it may not make you a millionaire. However, this book may serve as a supplemental learning tool that may clarify expectations of your future financial journeys, whether it's learning in a university or investing in the marketplace.

The information is this book covers a wide variety of topics. Some material may interest you, and some may not. The best way to approach this book is to take your time and reflect on the ideas and concepts. You are encouraged to take notes and review sections that are of interest to you. Later, if you decide to take a finance class, you can always refer back to this book for maximum results.

Finally, I have attempted to write this book as objectively as possible, but from time to time my opinions may appear. However, this should have a very limited effect on the main goals of the book, which are to demonstrate the necessity of finance; to clarify the definition, purpose, and goals of both finance and economics; to explore financial concepts using a simpler approach; and to attract more interest in this field. Happy reading!

# CHAPTER 1

# Introduction

## The Mother of Invention

There is an old saying: "necessity is the mother of invention". Throughout history it has seldom been proven false. Humans have made every tool and machine to meet their needs from the beginning of time. If we needed a tool to fish in order to eat, we made it. If we needed a pot to cook the fish in, we made it. When we needed a lot more fish to feed a larger population, we made a boat to take us to them. And so on until the present day, where we have every tool, machine, and form of transportation necessary to allow a human in one part of the world to eat a rare fish from another part of the world the day after it's caught.

This old saying can also be applied to finance. The subject was invented to fill the need of understanding of a subject that's entirely too important to ignore. In early civilizations humans performed all of life's required tasks alone. Each person was a one-stop shop. That is, a man built his own house, caught and cooked his own food, made his own clothes, etc.

This all changed as civilization progressed and work was spread out amongst many people. This was called the *division of labor*, and it created specialization. With division of labor, one man fished, another man hunted, and another man crafted the tools for each of these trades. A man could trade a day's labor of his specialty for a day's labor of another man's, for example a fisherman and a hunter. This process of bartering, along with division of labor, eventually gave birth to money to help facilitate the exchange. Between the time of bartering and the present, the need for understanding our complex monetary and wealth system has escalated to its highest point.

Now more than ever, there is a necessity to recognize the significance of finance. Now more than ever, there is a necessity to learn the science of finance.

## Finance and Science

Finance is not a traditional type of science compared to the natural sciences. When the average person thinks of traditional sciences he or she thinks of experiments conducted in isolated labs by scientists wearing white coats while bubbling glass tubes are displayed in the background. This is not the case for finance.

You can't physically dissect a balance sheet with a knife like you can an earthworm. You can dissect it mentally, though. You can't test financial ratios like you can with chemicals in beakers at various degrees of heat. However, you can perform calculations for the ratios and then interpret them based off knowledge of similar companies' financial positions from a historical perspective.

Thus finance is a unique science that needs to be explored with a different approach in order to find a better way to accomplish the unique goals of this field. For the sake of classification, many scholars list finance as a social science along with human behavior and economics. Some argue that social sciences are not real sciences. Again this all depends on your definition and goals of science. For every scientist in this world, there is a unique definition of science and the expectations that go along with it.

Science can be thought of as a progressive learning of a given subject. Alternatively, Albert Einstein, one of the most famous scientists in history, considered science a refinement of our daily thoughts. These are good starting interpretations; however, they are not complete. What is missing is the answer to the question "why?" That is, why are we trying to learn a given subject progressively? And why are we trying to refine our daily thoughts?

Another popular definition of science is "a persistent search for truth." Science *is* about searching for truth, but the search is only part of it. Thus, this definition does not answer the "why?" question either.

Why are we searching for truth? To answer this let's make a subtle change to our definition of science. The following statement will be the definition used in this book: **science is a**

**persistent search for a truly better way to perform an action or understand a condition, process, or thing.** This allows for all of the essential elements of the above definitions while providing a purpose. That is, science allows for progressive learning, refinement of our daily thoughts, and searching for truth in order to find a truly better way to perform an action or understand a condition, process, or thing.

This is more consistent with the belief that there is a science to everything. Searching for truth can be a quest relevant not only to the questions of the universe as a whole but to the questions of every little activity within our own everyday universe. All laborers in a free market are rewarded for finding faster and more effective ways to accomplish their tasks. *Thus everyone committed to persistently searching for better ways to do his or her job is a scientist in his or her own specialization.* Some examples are creating better ways to prepare food, listen to music or watch television, build houses, or catch fish, or even very simple jobs like stuffing envelopes.

The examples of science in action using the above definition are as creative as your imagination. If you can list a job, as boring as it may appear, it doesn't take much to imagine the laborer continuously reflecting on a better way to perform knowing that if he succeeds then he can make more money than the competition. This demonstrates the relationship between wealth and science: *the possibility of enhancing personal wealth has generally always been the carrot on the end of the stick enticing people to use their creativity to advance humanity. The possibility of enhancing personal wealth will also be the fuel to help the human race reach its maximum potential in the future.* If wealth has helped entice individual advancements in many specializations of science, wouldn't it make sense to create and analyze a science dealing with wealth? This is where finance comes in.

The science of finance is about finding better ways to manage wealth. Hence, by applying the definition of science to finance, which is the science of managing wealth for an individual, a group, or an organization, a more complete picture of it is now formed. **Finance has transformed into "a persistent search for truly better ways to manage wealth for an individual, a group, or an organization."** With this new definition we can appreciate finance as its own science, with its own goals to be achieved in a manner that works best for it.

The above general definition of science can be universally applied to all sciences. However, I don't agree that the methodology of every science should be the same, especially in the case of finance. A baker has customized methods of his or her science, and these methods cannot be compared fully to those of another science, for example anthropology. Various sciences are analogous to people in many ways, particularly in that they are unique. A glove may fit one person but it is not guaranteed that it will fit the next person. Thus, a different customized glove will need to be made. Similarly, the gloves of the scientific approach to other subjects, for example physics, may not fit the hand of finance. If that is the case, a new glove must be made.

Using traditional methods for sciences like finance and economics may result in the elimination of these sciences altogether and that would be tragic. Many of the greatest economists, including John Maynard Keynes and Friedrich Hayek, have noted the significance of economics for humanity. The same could be said for finance, as it follows paths similar to economics (the distinction will be analyzed later). *If you strip away the prospects of learning better ways to manage the wealth of a nation, as in economics, or the wealth of an individual, a group, or an organization, as in finance, our present wealth-dependent civilization might fully regress.*

If you subscribe to the belief that perfection is a journey and not a destination, you may also agree that there may never be a perfect way to do or understand something. Nevertheless, this does not eliminate the idea of searching for a better way. I know the above definition of science, which invites the notion that every laborer may be perceived as a scientist, may be very difficult for many to accept, particularly scientists in traditional branches who have been trained in specific protocols for collecting data, etc. They may feel this definition lowers their credibility because if everyone is a scientist then they may no longer be special. There is no reason to feel this way, as there are infinite amounts of ways in which individuals can be scientific. The only thing that changes is one word in the job title, for example an economic scientist versus a financial scientist.

Besides, not everyone will be scientists, only those who persistently search for better ways to perform an action or understand a condition, process, or thing. This new definition can help find a scientific place for subjects that are not traditional accepted as a science but can benefit from the search for better ways to perform their everyday tasks. Viewed from a different perspective, science as a whole benefits when all of its parts benefit.

# Where Is the Real Nobel Prize in Finance?

Now we have established a framework from which to view the science of finance. However, there still may be questions. To try and answer some of them, let's look at finance's history.

Finance as we know it, the so called modern finance, the stuff taught in schools, began with the 1950s economists, a line that has never been completely eliminated. Many of the originators of the basics of this subject have deep roots in various aspects of economics. For example Harry Markowitz, who mathematically explored portfolio selection, was an economist. His student William Sharpe, the founder of the CAPM theory amongst many other contributions to finance, is a microeconomist. Merton Miller and Franco Modigliani, founders of the famous M & M propositions for corporate finance are economists. Actually, Markowitz, Sharpe, and Miller all received a Nobel Prize in economics in 1990. Robert Merton and Myron Scholes, both considered financial economists, won the Nobel Prize in economics in 1997. Their work has also had a big impact on the content of finance and represents many of the theories that exist within it.

But where is the real Nobel Prize in finance? It doesn't exist unless you call it financial economics. Irrespective of whether the contributions of the founders of modern finance were beneficial to the field, it has very few who identify themselves solely in the science of finance. Most of the major contributors to finance consider themselves macroeconomists, microeconomists, financial economists, mathematicians, etc. There are very few, if any, who consider themselves scientists of finance or, to coin a term, *financialists*.

To some the problem may not be as apparent as it is to the students, instructors, and practitioners within this field. Economics is a very important subject but finance is not the same thing. There may have been points in earlier civilization where the distinction was blurred, but it's not anymore. Finance needs the respect it deserves as a separate subject, the kind that would get its own Nobel Prize category as opposed to hiding behind another similar subject. Finance is a serious subject, and the time has come for it to stand out completely on its own, not under the shadow of other subjects like economics.

Finance currently exists as a separate subject in universities mainly in form, and not entirely content and intent. There still exists a need for a completely independent science of finance that's recognized by all fields of scientists. In order to help distinguish the need for this subject and remove all barriers to respect as an independent science, in the next chapter we'll analyze what finance is.

# CHAPTER 2

# What Is Finance?

The concepts in this book, and every finance class you will ever take, will be useless unless you can at least acknowledge what finance is. The problem is that most financial textbooks today barely define it. The ones that do, generally give conflicting definitions, which is a big issue. If a clear, consistent definition of this subject is lacking, how can advancements in this field be made? No wonder many financial academics still call themselves financial economists instead of financialists.

Any solid building must have a solid foundation, and so it is with any scientific study. Clarifying the meaning of finance can help to secure it a better position in the field of scientific inquiry. If a consensus on the basic definition of finance cannot be attained, then I believe this field will continue to fall into an irreversible massive state of confusion.

Although there are many variations on the definition of finance, I believe the following is the most applicable: **finance is the science of management of wealth for an individual, a group, or an organization.** This statement has so much information packed into a few words. Let's analyze it further.

First and most important, finance is a unique and independent science, as we discussed in the "Introduction" chapter.

Second, management can be defined as the conducting of various activities for the purpose of meeting specific goals. In other words management must perform all actions necessary to meet their financial goals (hopefully in an ethical manner).

Third, this field pertains to the management of wealth.

Although I believe many financial academics may agree with my above definition of finance, defining wealth is not as easy to form a consensus on. At the simplest level, one can argue that money is wealth. But what is money? It's just a tool or a medium to exchange goods or services between one person and another. Without money our civilization would revert back to the days of bartering, for example, when one had two cows and wanted to exchange them for five fish. Bartering is a very inconvenient system. What if the ratio were one cow to two and a half fishes? A fish would have to be split in half to buy a cow.

Money was created because it is a much more convenient and overall effective method of trading goods or services. Money does store value; for example one thousand dollars can purchase you one thousand dollars' worth of goods and services. However, money as an asset, in all its various forms (for example cash),

10

is only one aspect of final wealth. A common misunderstanding in the study of finance is if you have a lot of money then you are wealthy. The problem with this statement is that it generally only looks at one specific type of asset, cash and its equivalents, and ignores many other assets like real estate. It also ignores debt (also known as liabilities). Many people in this world have plenty of money but a higher amount of debt. This situation can be very misleading. Although wealth can be stated in monetary form, money alone is not sufficient for an individual, a group, or an organization to be recognized as wealthy.

Wealth can also be defined as having a substantial amount of material possessions. This definition is a little more comprehensive than the one above because it includes most of the assets one owns. However, it does not include intangible assets that are commonly placed on balance sheets and may have significant value, e.g. copyrights, patents, and goodwill. More importantly this definition excludes liabilities. What good is having a whole bunch of assets if you have too much debt that can't be paid off? Inevitably, creditors will repossess all of those assets.

Let's look at this effect more closely with a little story of a rich man.

His name is John, and he drives around in very expensive cars. John has a $5 million house on the beach, and he dresses well, often wearing custom-made suits by the world's most famous designers.

John has a lavish lifestyle including frequent fancy dining and going on extravagant cruises to every corner of the globe. If you met him without knowing the details of his financial statements, it would be easy to conclude he is rich or wealthy (which mean the same thing). Based on the impression that John gives to the world he would be perceived as financially independent. However, perceptions can be illusionary.

Now let's suppose we have the opportunity to peek at John's financial statements, particularly the balance sheet. We discovered his total assets are worth $5 million. Based on that value alone, in a world where all other financial data is irrelevant, John is relatively wealthy compared to the average American. After further analysis, we also discovered John owes $25 million or five times as much as his total assets. In the real world, this is a big problem. John is a walking financial time bomb. He's probably using every part of his assets just to pay his creditors their interest. This can only endure until all of the assets are gone, either through depletion or bankruptcy. This is a prime example of why cash and other assets cannot be the true measuring stick of wealth. Debt must be included, or the perception of wealth of an individual, a group, or an organization can be an illusion.

This leads us to a better definition of wealth: the net worth of an individual, a group, or an organization. Net worth is total assets minus total liabilities as reflected on a balance sheet, one of the most important financial statements. We will be covering that later. In other words net worth is what's left over after you subtract everything you owe to creditors from everything you own. The degree to which the number is positive reflects how wealthy you are. If it's negative you are insolvent, a very bad financial state to be in. Few who venture into the dreadful land of insolvency may return. Large majorities never do, and end up legally bankrupt.

There are some problems with the above definition of wealth. For example, assets reflected on a balance sheet may not show the true market value if liquidated during an emergency. Thus a man may appear much wealthier than he would be if money were needed to pay off debts right now. Suppose an individual had 95 percent of his assets in real estate and needed to liquidate tomorrow to pay off creditors. Real estate is an illiquid asset, which means it may take a long time to sell and convert the asset to cash. This person may have to sell these assets for 30 to 50 percent (or less) than their worth to come up with the funding now.

Compare this situation to another person who has 95 percent of his assets in cash. If an emergency strikes, he is more likely to handle the situation better than the individual with mostly real estate. This is because most of his assets are already liquid, or easily convertible to cash. In fact, converting to cash is the essence of the definition of liquidity.

Another problem with defining wealth as an individual or organization's net worth is that it does not take into consideration one's expected level of net worth. This is an issue brought up by Dr. Thomas Stanley and Dr. William Danko in their book *The Millionaire Next Door*. For example, let's assume a surgeon has been making four times more money than a grade school teacher for thirty years. At the end of that period, if the surgeon ends up with roughly the same amount of wealth as the teacher, let's say $5 million, the surgeon should have earned much more, and did not meet his or her potential. Although the formula for calculating the expected level of net worth is debatable, it is safe to say the surgeon probably should have at least four times more wealth than the teacher at the end of the thirty years, assuming they have the same return on investments.

In this analysis, incorporating the expected level of net worth into the definition of wealth would be beneficial. However, this would entail a more complicated and highly debatable method, and my aim here is simplicity. Thus, for the purpose of this book, wealth will be defined only as the net worth of an individual, a group, or an organization.

Armed with this understanding of wealth, we can now say finance is the science of management of wealth for an individual, a group, or an organization, or *financial entities*. Managing wealth for an individual is the basis of personal finance, which includes only one person (and his or her family; please see the "Personal Finance" section in the "Types of Finance" chapter for more information). Groups will loosely include clubs, teams, or any smaller organizations. The major difference between groups and organizations is size and the general level of formality. Admittedly, these are loose definitions, but they're good enough for our purposes.

Organizations may be for-profit as well as nonprofit. Please note that even a nonprofit organization must focus on improving its wealth in order to funnel it toward its goals, such as cures for various diseases. If it doesn't operate in that regard, then, like any other organization, it may become insolvent, with unfulfilled goals. There will be more analysis on nonprofit organizations in other parts of this book.

Organizations can even include governmental departments and agencies but not a nation or a division of a nation, e.g., a city or state. **These organizations fall under the category of**

**economics, defined here as the science of management of wealth for a nation or a division of a nation.** This is a radical way of thinking about economics that can create ambiguity as to whether a particular governmental organization would fall under economics or finance. However, despite this limitation, I think this definition is the most effective to solidify the major distinctions between the two sciences. A detailed analysis of this will be explored further in the discussion of economics.

One final point on the definition of finance: it does not pertain only to investing. This is a common misconception held even by financial professionals and academics. Finance is a comprehensive subject that includes all aspects of managing wealth. Investing is a part of finance but not the entire purpose of it. For example, finance also includes managing cash that is not invested and risk-management techniques to preserve wealth by insurance. The science of finance uses a holistic approach to managing wealth, that is, by analyzing every aspect of it.

# CHAPTER 3

# The Purpose and Goals of Finance

**The purpose of finance is to continuously seek, analyze, and implement better ways to maximize wealth for an individual, a group, or an organization.** Note the word *continuously* above: building wealth is an ongoing process that never stops. It is very difficult to become wealthy through the fruits of one's own labor, and even harder to maintain it. Finance is more than learning how to create wealth; it is also learning how to ensure it is not lost.

There is an old saying that wealth is only as good as one's last investment. A person could be a successful investor for fifty plus years and become very wealthy. Suddenly he may make foolish decisions on an investment, and his wealth may regress to nil. All his life's savings would be lost in an instant from neglecting to implement intelligent actions learned from finance.

**The major goal of finance is to continuously maximize wealth for an individual, a group, or an organization.** Again note the word *continuously*. Maximization of wealth is not something that should be done solely for any random moment in time, for example by Friday, 5:00 p.m. EST, on December 31. To specify such is to imply that all other moments thereafter are irrelevant. To build wealth for one day and neglect it the next day, year, or decade is nonsensical. It must be an ongoing process.

The major goal of finance is comprehensive enough to include nonprofit organizations. Let me elaborate on why this is so. A nonprofit organization functions just like any other. It needs cash inflows to survive, and must pay cash out with that money. A nonprofit organization has bills too, for example, to keep its lights on. It may be different in how it receives funding, for example, via donations, but even a nonprofit strives to increase its assets and decrease its liabilities to the point of having the highest net worth possible. The big difference is that instead of paying out the profits to its owners, like a public company, it filters the money to a cause, for example, impoverished children in an underdeveloped country. Thus, aside from where the ultimate wealth is directed to, even a nonprofit organization should strive to maximize its wealth.

When a nonprofit doesn't focus on wealth maximization, it simply may start to accumulate debt and decrease assets. Yes, nonprofits can go broke too. Thus, anyone who studies finance, even nonprofit organizations, should be interested in finding better ways to maximize their wealth.

Philanthropists may be a potential limitation in the above goal. These are individuals who give their wealth away to charities. How can they be focused on maximizing wealth if they are also giving parts of it away? Philanthropists need to maximize their wealth for reasons very similar to those of nonprofit organizations. Instead of directing the proceeds to the owners' pockets, it is diverted to another cause, for example a charity. Philanthropists also have to ensure they don't give away more wealth than they can afford, or they will end up broke, and this would do no good for their charities.

Pretend you have a million dollars in wealth and you give it all away. Now there is no money left to help anyone else in the future. This is an extreme example demonstrating why even philanthropists need to strive to maximize their wealth. The more their wealth increases, the more they can afford to donate.

The major goal of finance is actually a final product of many smaller important goals, or *secondary goals*. Most people are excited by making money. Thus, the first secondary goal of finance is to maximize cash inflow. This can be in the form of a higher salary for an individual, or higher revenues for a corporation. Another goal may be to maximize profits. This goal is an extension of the first, as profits are what are left over from revenues after the expenses are paid.

A third goal is to minimize costs. If the costs can be reduced to close to zero, or zero if possible, that will enhance profits simultaneously. A fourth goal may be to reduce total liabilities. Debt can be helpful in certain circumstances; however, in general, no debt is preferable. If one can have all of their assets in place but make their debt magically disappear, that would be a major improvement of their financial position.

A fifth secondary goal of finance is to maximize assets ranging from everyday cash to real estate. A sixth goal may be to avoid bankruptcy, which is not considered an ideal situation for rational individuals, groups, or organizations. However, sometimes it may be necessary to improve a highly unfavorable financial position.

Another secondary goal of finance is to be financially independent, in other words, to have enough wealth to ensure that you can live life on your own terms. This goal is a part of the major goal of finance because continuously maximizing wealth for an individual may eventually lead to a state of financial independence.

These secondary goals are a small sample of other possible financial goals, some of which may be subjective in nature.

No goal of finance should be based on mere survival for any rational human being living in a modern civilization. In this sense the word *survival* means having just enough income to pay off expenses in order to exist. This does not include a situation where wealth is already built up and someone is living off the interest. A goal of mere survival, in other words, just living day to day or check to check, would conflict with the interest of any individual, group, or organization.

Every individual, group, or organization needs money to live and desires more money rather than less; consequentially, they also desire more wealth, as money is just a part of wealth. If they don't focus on increasing their money and their overall wealth, the alternative is to survive poorly. For example, if one chooses not to work and have income, she may lose her house and become homeless. At the individual level, although there are people who appear indifferent to maximizing their wealth and want to exist just to pay their bills, if they fully thought through the argument, I believe, they would easily convert their opinions. For example, if a person were financially struggling his whole life and an opportunity presented itself to improve his position and assist him in avoiding future financial struggles, it would be almost suicidal, and certainly foolish, to decline this offer and choose to continue the more painful path of more resistance. **In short, in our modern civilization, to struggle financially means to struggle in every aspect of life.**

# CHAPTER 4

# The Financial Manager

**A financial manager is an individual who manages wealth for an individual, a group, or an organization.** At the personal level, anyone who pays a bill or receives some form of compensation, whether it is a salary or a commission, is a financial manager to a degree. The more bills one pays and the more income one manages, the more one's activities mirror a fully active financial manager. A head of a busy household is a prime example. He collects various incomes and pays out various expenses such as utility bills. He also strives to fulfill the major goal of personal finance: to continuously maximize wealth for an individual or a family. This can be achieved by increasing assets while paying off debt.

As the group size increases, and the group becomes a more formal organization, generally the role of the financial manager shifts to include different types of responsibilities. Larger organizations may need more than one financial manager to perform all required tasks. For-profit organizations such as corporations may have financial managers focus on meeting the financial goals of the owners of the company. This may create an agency problem that will be explored in a future chapter titled "The Agency Problem".

The financial managers of a nonprofit organization focus on meeting the financial goals of the organization so they can pass more wealth to its cause. Without financial managers none of the goals for an individual, a group, or an organization would be met. These managers should study finance in order to maximize the probability of meeting their goals or the goals of their clients.

# CHAPTER 5

# The Financialist and the Financier

It is time to clarify a few important terms for people who are connected to the science of finance. In every science there needs to be a specialist. That is where the financialist comes into play. **A financialist is a scientist who specializes in the science of finance.** Although on rare occasions this term has been used ambiguously, it finally has a place to call home. A financialist is a very important individual whose job is to search persistently for a truly better way to manage wealth for an individual, a group, or an organization.

The time for financialists to be given respect is long overdue. The science of economics has a name for its specialists called *economists*. The two fields, economics and finance, are similar in many ways, yet they are clearly separate sciences. Thus they need separate specialists.

Economists should study economics. Financialists should study finance. There is no reason why economists who specialize in managing the wealth of nations, should be the dominating experts in a science that deals with wealth management from the perspective of an individual, a group, or an organization. This job should be left to the financialist. This is made clear in a popular economic concept discussed by Adam Smith in *The Wealth of Nations*, called the *division of labor*. This stipulates that if each person focuses his time and energy on one specific task, he may gain maximum efficiency of that task compared to others who focus on a different task.

Although the two sciences are separate, it is possible for one scientist to be both a financialist and an economist at the same time. This would require a tremendous amount of research and preparation, as he would have to study two separate sciences. This would all depend on his ambitions and how much work he can manage. Someone could be a scientist in both sciences the same way that someone can become a medical scientist and a legal scientist simultaneously. However, it may be more realistic for each scientist to focus only on one specialty.

The next term to clarify is *financier*. This word has been used frequently as of late, yet it is still ambiguous. *Financier* and *financial manager* tend to mean the same thing when used colloquially. However, a financial manager, as we've defined, is an individual who manages wealth for an individual, a group, or an organization. **A financier is an individual who manages *large levels* of wealth for an individual, a group, or an**

**organization.** The main difference here is size. A financial manager can be anyone from a head of a household for a family of average wealth to an employee of a large corporation. On the other hand, a financier is an individual who *only* manages large levels of wealth, a term we will define only loosely for now. Thus a financier is a specific type of financial manager, just as a speculator is a specific type of investor. Please see the "Investing Overview" chapter for more on this.

A financier might also be an investor, but the role is more comprehensive than that. A financier's focus is to manage not only investments but all parts of wealth including income, debts, insurance, etc. The main goal is to maximize wealth using all financial tools available. Thus a financier is commonly defined as only an investor or investment manager, although that conflicts with the above definition. A financier is not just an investor.

Financialists and financial managers (especially financiers) are important members of finance. Financialists study the science academically while financial managers are the practitioners. Both parties have equally important roles: the financialist derives academically better ways to manage wealth and the practitioner implements the techniques. Financial managers are on the front line, confronting theory versus reality on a daily basis. Their knowledge is invaluable to the field.

Ultimately the best financialists are individuals who are also active financial managers or financiers. Financialists are encouraged to be hands-on and conduct experiments in the financial fields of everyday markets in order to know what finance is like in practice. What good are creating models and theories that have no correlation to what is happening in reality? If a financialist is also a financial manager, then he can test theories when applicable. As the old saying goes, it takes one to know one. A great financialist will practice what he preaches to be sure financial academia and reality are aligned well.

# CHAPTER 6

# A Digression on Money

To recall, money is just a tool to exchange for various goods and services. The result of money is an established price mechanism that can assist people in conducting their daily business. In simple terms, money makes everyday life easier to manage.

As money is just a symbol of stored wealth, it can be in the form of anything including paper, gold, silver, sea shells, rocks, even alcohol and cigarettes (as occurred after World War II in Germany). *It doesn't matter what the object is that represents money. What matters is the belief in what money can do.*

As long as people believe a specific symbol, whether tangible or intangible, is fit to trade for goods or services, it will endure. Without the belief in the quality of the symbol, the monetary system may collapse and be exchanged for another.

# CHAPTER 7

# The History of Finance

## In the Beginning

The birth of finance occurred long before humans realized it. However, the actual time frame is highly subjective. The following analysis is my interpretation of the history of finance. I admit it is brief and may be incomplete. However, I have included it here as a framework.

When analyzing finance, a major question is: how far back should we go? The answer depends on what part of the world we're referred to. The roots of finance could have started back in the earliest civilizations in all parts of the world. If we can identify any component of wealth as defined in this text, for example assets or liabilities, in prior civilizations, we have a good reference point.

Many historians consider the hunter-gatherer phase to be the first state of civilization. In this state money is not necessary, as people do everything themselves: they hunt and cook their own food, and make their own shelters. There is little coordination with any other groups of people, thus little need to trade. They may barter on occasion when encountering another tribe, but this may not have been the norm. Basically, in this older civilization, people were fully independent of society, and their own talents to survive may have been their biggest assets. If we can accept the human talent of survival as an asset, we can say this period is a good starting point in our analysis of the history of finance.

## Making Progress

Eventually, humans domesticated their animals and became wandering shepherds. With domestication humans did not need to hunt much, as food was readily available. This opened up opportunities for bringing more people together, as more people can be fed with an available stock of domesticated animals.

Inevitably shepherds stopped wandering and settled down to become farmers. A stable farmer with a stable group of animals equated to even more available food. For example a stock of chickens would provide a ready supply of eggs, and cows a ready supply of milk. Also farmers grew their own crops, which may have increased the supply of desirable fruits, vegetables, and spices. This created an opportunity for more bartering than before. More people lived together, as there was easier access to food.

Bartering, or trading, is the predecessor of a monetary system. How else can people exchange labor if money has not been invented yet? Think of a fisherman who spends ten plus hours a day catching fish. He may catch enough fish to feed one hundred people, certainly much more than his wife and children can consume before it becomes inedible. It would be a waste to throw away the fish his family cannot consume. Instead the man takes what he needs to feed his family and trades the rest to someone else who has spent many hours of labor on a different specialty, for example pottery.

In a bartering system, one can trade, a large water jug for a few fish. However, in this system it is very difficult to quantify how many hours of labor would equate to the same amount of labor for another job. What if the fisherman catches one hundred fish each day, assuming the same amount of hourly labor, but some days the fish are very small and other days they are very large? Let's pretend the exchange rate is five fish for one wine jug, and the fisherman and jug maker complete two exchanges on separate days. The first exchange goes well. However, for the second exchange the fish are very small, and the jug maker feels cheated. He may desire the larger fish he received in the first transaction. Even though the fisherman worked the same amount of hours, his fish came up small on the second round, which may be no fault of his. Without money there is an inefficient price system that results in plenty of opportunity for injustice, as this example illustrates.

How could money fix this situation? The fish may be priced at $10 a pound. The price of the jug may be fixed at $10 for the standard large size. Now the two laborers can trade goods more easily. If the fisherman has a bad day and catches smaller fish, it is still $10 a pound. The jug maker can be assured his standard large jug can be fairly traded for a consistent weight of fish every time. That is, a $10 pound of fish always buys a $10 wine jug.

## Early Currency

Eventually a state of human civilization analogous to the ancient Egyptians' was reached. Ancient Egyptians are not known to have used coins but did use money in other forms, for example gold and silver jewelry. They may have started to realize that using symbols to exchange goods and services makes doing business much easier. This set humans on a search for an even better way to improve the existing primitive versions of money.

The creation of the coin was a revolutionary step in finance. It demonstrated that money was working as a system to exchange goods and services. This knowledge led the quest for refining the existing currency. As of the time of this writing, although the specific date is debatable, it's generally considered that the first coins were produced around the eighth century BC. Coins were initially used by earlier civilizations such as the ancient Chinese, Indians, and Persians. Who invented the coin first is still a mystery archaeologists may one day discover. Eventually the ancient Greeks and Romans improved on coin making. As time progressed the use of coins became more complex, and the stamps on them more elaborate.

Money also became divisible into various units of exchange. This allowed a seller to give change to a buyer and created a more just monetary system. Coins proved to be a highly successful tool to facilitate the process of managing wealth.

## A Note on Debt

The invention of debt is another highly debatable event. It probably occurred as far back as the bartering system. Using our previous example, let's suppose the jug maker falls ill for a month and needs food. If he has an established relationship with the fisherman and is known to be an honest person, the fisherman may give the jug maker a few fish while he is sick. This would prevent the jug maker and his family from starving. In return the jug maker could promise to make some elaborate jugs or other pottery for the fisherman once he is able to return to work.

This action is the essence of debt. The jug maker now owes the fisherman goods. This transaction also demonstrates what money in its purest form represents: an exchange of one's labor for that of another. The jug maker owes a mutually acceptable amount of his labor (debt) in exchange for the lent labor of the fisherman.

## Other Financial Events

Many major developments in finance occurred during the Renaissance (roughly the twelfth to the early seventeenth century AD). To understand what happened, let's examine a few historical points. First, Arabic numbers were used in substitute for the older Roman numerals. This was a significant improvement in efficiency when performing basic business math calculations. Second, Christianity did not permit the lending of money for the purposes of earning interest, or what was called *usury*. The Jewish people who lived in Italy at the time were the only ones allowed to perform this activity, and they conducted their business on a bench, *la banca* in Italian, and the origin of the word *bank*. If someone didn't like the way a lender did business, then he would break his bench, *bancarotta* in Italian, the origin of the word *bankrupt*.

The Medici family in Italy during the Renaissance became the driving force that led to banking as it is known today. The Medicis found a creative loophole that allowed them to lend money and avoid the existing usury laws. Their banking operation became extremely successful; they lent money all over Europe. This period spurred a quest for better ways to perform banking activities.

With the birth of banking, finance was changed forever and managing wealth took on a whole new meaning. The invention of the banking system led people to think of better ways to use debt to obtain more wealth quickly. However, it was probably immediately obvious that debt is a double-edged sword. If used properly it can magnify one's gains; if used improperly it can magnify losses.

Another historical development was the use of stocks. The East India Companies in the 1600s were the first stock companies. The stock market eventually evolved, and the idea was carried to the United States, where the first stock market formed in

Philadelphia in 1790. Since then it's transformed into a platform where anyone can trade any public stock in real time.

Most other major developments happened in the twentieth century. They include, but are not limited to, the creation of the credit card, the mutual fund, the index mutual fund, the exchange-traded fund, and various derivatives. It is still debatable whether some of these innovations have helped or hurt society.

Finance has been evolving over thousands of years. More elaborate forms of assets and debt have been created, along with a monetary system to carry it forward. Combine these with one of the most business-friendly economies that ever existed, and it becomes necessary to study wealth and the management of it.

## Historical Perspectives of Wealth

The management of wealth started in the earliest civilizations. Each civilization defined wealth differently, and approached finance from a different viewpoint. Wealth generally meant intangible assets to the hunters. A person who can hunt better than anyone else is worth more than any piece of gold. Consider why the early Native Americans could not understand the infatuation the Spanish had with gold. To these people gold did not have much value. They preferred to spend their time managing their survival skills, which translated to finance for them, as they were managing what they perceived was wealth.

The management of wealth was also different for the shepherd civilizations. For these people wealth consisted of the animals they tended to daily, whether it was sheep, reindeer, cows, or chicken. When the shepherds stopped roaming and became stable farmers, more secure homes were considered wealth.

The main point is that as civilization advanced through its many stages, the definition of wealth as presented in this book became more relevant. In a hunter civilization, our definition would have had limited value for several reasons. First, these individuals had limited bartering, thus almost no opportunity to owe anyone anything. For them debt was almost irrelevant. Second, a large majority of the current categories of assets did not exist, for example cash, mutual funds, stocks, and bonds. Thus their wealth, as defined here as net worth, was basically the sum of everything they considered an asset. As noted above, their perception of an asset was completely different from how it is in modern civilization. Nevertheless, anything perceived to be an asset was an opportunity for management, thus a need for finance emerged in its primitive form.

# CHAPTER 8

# Modern Finance

## Founding Fathers

We can bring our examination of the history of finance full circle with an analysis of how modern finance, as currently taught in universities, came to be. First let's review its academic aspects. Various phrases about wealth can be found in the Old Testament of the Bible and in writings by various Greek and Roman historians. Benjamin Franklin wrote *Poor Richard's Almanac* from 1733 to 1758, which demonstrated true reflections on individual wealth. Franklin captured a collection of phrases from throughout the ages that illustrated how the seeds of finance had started to sprout as people thought about ways to improve their financial situations.

A big shift of thinking on wealth came about with Adam Smith's *The Wealth of Nations* in 1776. Many consider Smith the father of economics; considering the topics he explored in his book, it may be even argued that he is the founder of modern finance. *The Wealth of Nations* looked at the economy from a top-down as well as a bottom-up approach. That is, Smith considered the wealth problems of nations while also reflecting on the wealth problems of the individual. His book was such a success it became the footnote to almost every economics book published after it. However, he is not given credit for having any connection to finance in current financial textbooks.

Fast forwarding about one and a half centuries, Benjamin Graham was another pioneer in the area of finance who is often not given proper credit. Graham was known for his analyses of various financial instruments called *securities*; thus he was the founder of *security analysis*. He wrote two major books: *Security Analysis* in 1934 and *The Intelligent Investor* in 1949. These were major contributions to finance and had monumental impacts on many successful investors, including John Bogle and Warren Buffett.

To understand Graham's contribution to finance it is necessary to understand what a security is. A security is generally considered a specific type of an investment. It is usually more regulated than those not considered as a security by law. It includes many of the existing modern investments, such as stocks, bonds, and options. By buying securities, assuming that debt is not increased in order to fulfill the transaction, the purchaser may increase her assets position and total wealth. Graham, by analyzing investments that would have positive or negative effects on wealth, walked within the scope of finance as defined in this book. He did not explore every aspect of finance, as there are many more to consider when managing wealth. Yet he explored one of the most popular aspects: security analysis. For this contribution, it also may be argued, he is the founder of modern finance.

Many modern textbooks and universities recognize that modern finance originated with several economists starting in the 1950s. First Harry Markowitz produced an article called "Portfolio Selection" in 1952. His ideas began a wave of financial theories up until the present, and led to the formalizing of the subject now taught at universities as finance. Before Markowitz's time, if you wanted to study finance it would have been guised under different subject names like bookkeeping (old-fashioned accounting), economics, or general business.

William Sharpe, a student of Markowitz, later contributed to this new field with two major articles. In one, he explored the capital asset pricing model (CAPM), one of the most widely discussed financial models in finance classes today. CAPM set the foundation for modern finance as it allowed a framework for analyzing risk and return as it relates to the marketplace. This model was improved throughout the years. Eventually an alternative method was created by Stephen Ross in 1976, called the arbitrage pricing theory (APT).

There are just a few more names and events that need to be mentioned before this discussion can come together. Two more famous economists were analyzing finance at the corporate level. Franco Modigliani and Merton Miller put together two articles in

1958 and 1961, which formed the famous M and M propositions that dealt with the ideal capital structure for a company (this will be explained later). Their analysis created a debate that is still ongoing today. It entails determining the proportion of debt and equity a company should use when it needs funds.

Eugene Fama, also considered a founder of modern finance by many textbook authors and universities, made several contributions to the theoretical aspects of finance. He produced articles in the 1960s and 1970s that discussed two concepts that are at the heart of many financial discussions today: random walk and the efficient market hypothesis (EMH). In short his works implied that stock price movements are unpredictable and follow a *random walk*. His EMH proposed three types of efficiency for the market: strong, semi-strong, and weak.

Many others have contributed to the field of finance since Markowitz and are well recognized in various finance textbooks. They include, but are not limited to: Robert Merton, Myron Scholes, Fischer Black, and Robert Shiller.

## Finance Is Not Economics

So after this detailed review of the history of finance, it's obvious that the debate on who founded modern finance is questionable. I think naming a founding father is too subjective and will lead nowhere. Too many people have contributed to the field in their own unique ways, and it is the summation of all of these different contributions that has created a name for this field and led to this book. Every one of the names above should be given credit as a major contributor to finance. *However, the focus should be less on who founded the science and more on what the science is about and where do we go from here.*

Finance has its roots in the earliest parts of civilization. There are so many contributors whose names will never be known. They have as much right to be called founding fathers as anyone else, but because their names and works were not etched in stone and are not studied at modern universities, they receive no recognition. Thus, it is better if more energy is spent on productive activities like building a respectable science than wasting energy on an argument that is inconclusive.

With the modern history of finance presented above, it is possible to view the problem addressed in this book in a clearer light. Since the time of Harry Markowitz, an economist, most if not all of the founders of modern finance have been economists. Thus, its concepts have been created out of the shadows of economics. From its origination the field has slowly drifted until the present, where the subject is filled with many theories yet is improperly defined from one textbook to the next.

More evidence of this ambiguity is reflected by the Nobel Prizes in economics awarded to Markowitz, Sharpe, and Miller in 1990 for their pioneering work in financial economics. Based on the definitions in this book, it is clear one can refer to either finance or economics, but not both. In 1997 more Nobel prizes were awarded to Robert Merton and Myron Scholes for finding a new method to determine derivatives, an investment type dealing with the management of wealth for an individual, a group, or an organization. Of course a nation should be concerned with how that will eventually translate to the wealth of the whole society if those derivative markets happen to spiral out of control and cause a financial meltdown. However, the nature of Merton and Scholes's award is another example of the confusion that still exists about the distinction between finance and economics. Considering that these Nobel Prize winners have made contributions to the financial field and are mostly recognized in finance textbooks and not economics, their contributions, using the definition in the book, should be rightly attributed to the proper science.

As it is, finance professors are stuck teaching a science without proper merit, nor even a clear consistent distinction of what their field is. However, this is not just an issue for finance professors but for many current and future finance students. How many more finance degrees will be awarded to students in a field where the subject's definition, purpose, and goals are still obscure?

Milton Friedman, a famous economist, had it all right from the beginning. Friedman was Markowitz's professor at the University of Chicago. He argued that Markowitz should not earn his PhD in economics for his dissertation about portfolio selection, which was not about economics. Markowitz's dissertation was the turning point that began the new field of finance. Friedman understood this difference all along: **economics is not finance and finance is not economics.**

# CHAPTER 9

# Who Needs Finance?

## Money and Wealth Are Inescapable

The science of finance is necessary for everyone. **Every individual, group, organization, and country (in the case of economics) in modern civilization needs money, and consequently wealth, to survive.** Thinking of a situation where money would be irrelevant to function today takes much imagination. It can be argued that you don't need money if you move out into the wilderness and live off the land. That may be true until the owner of that land decides to build condos. You will then need to find other land off of which to live. Alternatively, you can build wealth to buy your own land and avoid this situation from reoccurring. Admittedly, it is possible for talented squatters to live many years, possibly a lifetime, for free on another's property. However, with land becoming scarcer every day, these elite squatters may eventually become extinct.

It may also be argued one does not need money if one goes to prison for life. Yes, in prison money is helpful, but not necessary. However, wealth is still relevant if one considers all of the human talent, an asset, which an individual will be deprived of sharing with the world for such a tradeoff. In finance this is called an *opportunity cost*, or the price one pays for choosing one event over another. If the person in question didn't go to prison for life, he might have had a successful career and became very wealthy. Instead his freedom and success are exchanged for the security of a lifetime of free room and board. Also consider that in this situation, although the prisoner does not spend money, citizen's tax money is spent on him. Someone has to pay for the prisoner to be fed, sheltered, and monitored. I call this a classic case of *financial survival by a third party*. Many examples fall within this category, such as dependent children who don't need money because their parents pay for everything.

A person may also claim that he doesn't need money because he is very spiritual and doesn't believe in money. However, this argument will only last until the bill collectors aren't paid. It will be a quick wakeup call when the electric, gas, and water service are shut off, the landlord starts an eviction process, and no food has been purchased to eat. The result will be a starving homeless person. Despite its suicidal nature, one may be willing to endure this consequence if he really doesn't believe in money. However, when he is responsible for a family, he will have to witness his partner and children suffering the same fate, which might be a more difficult event to endure. The only way for this person to undo this situation and support his family is to admit the significance of increasing his wealth.

There are many more creative situations where one can argue that money or wealth is not needed to survive. However, realistically, in a modern civilization, money and wealth are inescapable parts of life and counterarguments will eventually meet the same fate as the ones above.

## A Condition for Individual Survival

We have now established that everyone in our modern civilization needs wealth, including money, for survival. Consequently, finance, the science of management of wealth for an individual, a group, or an organization, also becomes necessary. All individuals need to manage their cash and other assets while guarding against excessive debt in order to maximize their wealth. An individual who strives to maximize her wealth indirectly maximizes her chances of successful survival. The more wealth she has, the lower the probability of her family starving or being homeless. Of course other factors can impact one's survival as well, even if one is technically rich, for example war, natural disasters, and a self-destructive personality. Nevertheless, assuming these factors are irrelevant, wealth is a major determining factor, arguably the most important factor for survival. **Thus the management of wealth in order to meet the goal of continuously maximizing wealth becomes a condition for individual survival.**

What applies to an individual in this analysis also applies to a group or an organization. After all groups and organizations are collections of people coming together to meet goals. If a group, for example a social club, doesn't pay its expenses, it will be difficult for it to continue its existence. These expenses may include the cost of renting space to hold meetings and various social functions.

Organizations also need to manage their wealth in order to survive. For example, if a company does not manage its debt properly it may quickly become insolvent. This may result in a quick dissolution of the company as it can no longer afford to survive. It doesn't matter what business you're in; wealth management must be considered as a priority in everyday activities. If the financial managers of a business are indifferent to this, they may eventually find their company extinct. Organizations must continuously find better ways to increase their incomes and minimize their costs and debts. **Ignoring the lessons of finance equates to welcoming a lifetime of financial struggles for an individual, a group, or an organization.**

## CHAPTER 10

# Finance Misunderstood

Throughout my career I have often been amazed by how many people don't understand what finance is. However, the most amazing part is that many people who should understand it do not. For example, there are various financial professionals, including but not limited to insurance agents, bankers, security brokers, real estate professionals, private lenders, and investment specialists, who don't understand why they are financial professionals. It may be safe to assume that your average financial professional doesn't even have a clear understanding of the basic components of wealth. The sad part is this happens at all levels of the managerial spectrum. I have met presidents and vice presidents of banks who, when I said I teach finance, actually responded: "You teach finance? What is that?"

Please let me clarify the underlying problem here. There are many individuals whose jobs are to manage the wealth of banks, institutions whose daily decisions can have exponential effects on their customers' wealth and on society at large. Yet these financial managers do not understand the definition, purpose, or goals of the field in which they operate. That is equivalent to a nurse, medical doctor, or a surgeon not understanding what the purpose of the health field is. Can you imagine any one of these professionals asking a medical professor for more clarification? "You teach health sciences? What is that?" Any intelligent patient who overheard that conversation would find another health professional quickly if they knew what was best for them.

I am not trying to single out anyone in particular for this discussion. This has just been the result of my experience. During my career I have met with financial professionals from all over the country and have often encountered the same situation. Many of them do have a good understanding of what finance is. However, it appears to be as inconsistent as the textbooks they read when learning the subject. This is nobody's fault in particular. Nonetheless, until there is a consistent understanding of the fundamental differences of finance this science will never be given full credit.

Many of the practitioners in this field hold finance degrees and must be able to explain to a client, without hesitation, the general nature of what they studied in school. If they cannot do this their clients may form negative impressions of the subject, which will continue to fuel negative credibility for the science as well as the financial industry. This also applies to financial academics. Finance professors across the world should have consistent responses when explaining their field to students. For a more in-depth analysis of what these responses should be, please review the chapter "What Is Finance?" earlier in this book. Finance has developed to the point where it cannot continue any longer in its current form without a consistent agreement on the basics of this science.

## CHAPTER 11

# The Significance of a Financial Education

If everyone in modern civilization needs finance, it would be in their best interest to pursue a financial education. Finance is a topic everyone needs to learn at least the basics of in order to better their chances of survival. This does not mean everyone should become finance majors or professionals. This simply means those who are interested in meeting their financial goals should find ways to become more educated in this field.

Finance students have many options for increasing their financial education. They can learn from reading books, working with tutors, attending universities or colleges, working with knowledgeable friends or family members, joining investment clubs, or even attending local investment workshops.

As finance can get very complicated at advanced levels, it is more sensible for students to master the basics before pursuing more challenging topics. The average person whose field is not financially related may only need to concentrate on the fundamentals of finance. Learning basic ways to manage wealth may improve one's financial position and have very rewarding results for people of all occupations. The fundamentals may help someone gain an appreciation of the potential rewards one may earn from mastering this field.

If a student jumps too fast into the advanced aspects of finance, he may suddenly lose all interest, and it might be hard to regain. Thus, the effect could be lost potential long-term wealth. One should explore finance slowly, at a pace that is comfortable to the student.

There is another way to obtain a financial education, and this occurs simply from being alive. Just by being a part of modern civilization you may obtain a financial education in various forms. However, that does not mean you will understand the financial education life tosses at you on a daily basis. Interpreting these financial lessons of life requires a significant time commitment. Each financial mistake needs to be dissected to understand where you went wrong in order not to make that mistake again. The more financial mistakes that can be avoided, the higher the probability of financial success.

It can be argued that it is not necessary to read financial books or learn finance in school because this kind of knowledge can be learned for free during life's lessons. This statement is a dangerous fallacy to buy into. If a person makes a financial mistake without studying the subject, the lesson is not free. Actually in some cases, it could cost the individual his only opportunity for fortune in his life. If one obtains a financial education before he makes a mistake, he may not only avoid the mistake but also make a wiser and more profitable decision.

It is also important to consider the length of time a financial lesson may be learned academically versus through everyday living. Many lessons can be learned faster through studying them. Many can be learned faster by living them. There is no set formula for this; it varies based on the outcomes of an individual's life and preferred learning methods. For example, you may quickly figure out how to use money for daily transactions, such as writing checks and investing in a bank savings account, by paying a visit to a local bank and asking about their products. However, you may never have an opportunity to learn other aspects of finance, like how the stock market works, until you study them.

An academic financial education combined with life's financial lessons presents an optimal situation to master the concepts. There are opportunities to practice finance everywhere. After studying concepts in finance, you can explore them further by testing the knowledge in the real world, this science's experimental field. For example, if you are learning about the stock market in school, you can invest a small amount (maybe $100) into a stock after doing much research, just to be engaged with the subject. The ideal result is to get a maximum education with as little amount possible lost to investing. A varied education might help you avoid negative outcomes that might occur otherwise.

To conclude, gaining some form of financial education can be very beneficial. This can be in addition to the financial education offered by living in our modern society. The combination of an academic financial education and life's financial education can create the maximum probability of financial success. If one can learn about the various concepts by practicing them via exercises, for example in a university, in addition to finding ways to make finance practical in the real world, he can obtain a better understanding of the subject. This can help him make more productive financial decisions and avoid very costly financial mistakes.

# CHAPTER 12

# Why Is Finance Exciting?

I get mixed emotional responses from people when I tell them I teach finance. Many people seem bewildered because finance is perceived as mysterious and complicated. More than likely if I stated I teach physics, also considered mysterious and complicated by many people, I would get the same reaction. I suspect finance is thought of this way because I generally don't hear any more questions after I mention the subject. Occasionally I get a response like, "Does that have anything to do with lending money?" Or, "Is that the same thing as an MBA?" Well, I guess, they're partially correct, but these questions are the exception. Most of the time their expressions are blank and their mouths are looking for words.

I have also found many people equate finance with being boring. Many have told me they don't want to learn about finance because it is probably really uninteresting. I have heard stories from people who read finance books to help them fall asleep at night. Some have even said it takes as little as five minutes of reading. If this really works, I think it may be great for the medical community.

I will admit there may be some areas of finance that are a little dull compared to others. However, it doesn't have to be this way. Finance is a subject as alive as life itself. I started studying it at an early age because I realized the significance of the problems it addresses. **Understanding finance is about maximizing one's chance of survival. What is more important than learning how to survive?**

The early hunters thought that surviving in the wilderness was an asset, thus finance to them was managing this skill. In modern civilization the hunter's dangerous wilderness has been replaced by a background of modern skyscrapers representing the corporate world, and the skill set required to survive has increased. People now need to know how to manage wealth to maximize it. Sure, it doesn't hurt to know how to catch your own food, cook it, and then eat it in a shelter you have built. However, it is money and other forms of wealth that allow one to live comfortably in our society. One does not need to catch and cook his own food, as he can go buy it at a grocery store or restaurant if he has money. One does not need to build his own shelter, as he can pay someone else to do it for him, if he has money. It is money, earned mostly from one's labor (or someone else's, as in the cases of gifts and inheritances), and the management of it that will allow comfortable survival to continue.

**Simply, finance today is about life and death.** So how many other subjects can be as important? There are a few, but not many. These may include economics, medical sciences, martial sciences, and the law (though only as it applies to life-and-death situations). There are some others, but they do not deal with such serious circumstances.

To understand the extent of the severity of finance, consider a financial professional's role compared to that of a surgeon. If a surgeon makes a mistake then the patient can die. However, if a financial professional, e.g. a stock broker, invests and loses all of his client's retirement money one week before the client is to retire, he may have done more harm than the surgeon. This client may now be considered in a state worse than death, a living death called *being broke*. That alone is difficult. Being broke after a lifetime of hard work because someone you blindly trusted put your money in the wrong investment is unbearable. Some do choose suicide after this occurs, and some choose therapy. There is no doubt this situation can be as serious as life itself.

If finance is one of the most important subjects that exists, it should not be classified as boring. There are many things that excite people, all of them highly subjective. For example a toy bear will excite a three-year-old but is unlikely to have the same effect on a twenty-three-year old. Nevertheless, there are certain subjects that excite people across the board. Making money is certainly one of them. Increasing wealth excites people of all ages. Even little children get excited when they are given cash or coins to do whatever they want with it. After a few experiences at a store, the children quickly learn the value of money and what

X amount can buy. The cycle has started, and they generally will desire more.

Thus, it can be concluded that if obtaining money is exciting, the whole science pertaining to it should also be exciting. However, even with all of the information presented, many people are indifferent to learning even the basics of the subject. Many think it is too complicated and do not want to tackle the challenge. What is more painful: to endure many years of financial struggles or to spend some time mastering the basics of finance to help increase your probability of being financially independent? If studying finance can help improve your financial position then it should be considered worth it in the long run.

Finance is exciting! This subject encompasses more than just fundamentals. It is alive every day in the news you read. Current events help provide unique financial scenarios to analyze for future growth. There is always a news line to help a financial student rethink what she has learned in order to master the management of her own wealth. Finance does not have to be as boring as many perceive it to be.

There are difficult problems in the field, but not every financial problem concerns everybody. Some are more applicable to those who specialize in that branch of finance. For example, problems that relate to trading corporate bonds are more appropriate for bond traders than for real estate investors. A student of finance has to find what he wants to learn to make the most out of the experience. It does not matter what your occupation is; you can customize the concepts of finance to assist with your interests and your business. Finance is as exciting as the student wants to make it!

# CHAPTER 13

# What Is Economics?

It is extremely important that the distinction between finance and economics is fully clear before we move forward. For an analysis of what finance is, please review the "What Is Finance?" chapter above.

It is time to discuss economics in order to complete the analysis. Please note that the following discussion is short in order to stay focused on the goals of this book.

It is absolutely amazing that economics faces the same problems as finance. In many textbooks authors don't even attempt to define economics before entering into a discussion of the subject. There are many textbooks with one thousand plus pages of content but no clear definition of economics. When definitions are offered, they are not consistent from text to text. The same problem occurs with how economics is taught at many universities.

The interesting part about this is that economics has a longer formal academic history than finance. Modern economics can be said to have started with Adam Smith's publication of *The Wealth of Nations* in 1776. It could also have started when David Ricardo published *On the Principles of Political Economy and Taxation* in 1817, his attempt to formalize the subject. Thus, compared with modern finance's recent beginnings in the 1950s, modern economics had a big head start to organize its science. Nevertheless, it lacks consistent clarity of its definition, purpose, and goals.

Despite this, the science has exploded, with different specialized fields of study. The field of economics includes, but is not limited to, macroeconomics, microeconomics, financial economics, urban economics, public economics, labor and demographic economics, international economics, agricultural and natural resource economics, and environmental and ecological economics. It covers topics all across the board, including but not limited to inflation, unemployment, population control, union wages, health insurance, taxation, national debt, tariffs, trade embargos, government price fixing, monetary and fiscal policy, imports and exports, minimum wages, and rent control. Considering all of these different fields and topics that have become categorized as parts of economics, it may be very surprising that the science itself is not clearly defined. Thus, it has the same problems that are rooted in finance.

It has recently occurred to me that while I'm writing this book to define and distinguish finance clearly, a secondary unintentional effect may also be produced: this book may serve as a guiding point to define clearly the nature, purpose, and goals of economics. To my knowledge, this clarification has never been done for economics in the manner in this book. Thus, if economists adopt the following approach to defining their field, they may find their field more organized, which will help to add clarity for future advancement of the science.

When I thought about how economics could be distinguished from finance, I realized Adam Smith had it right all along with the title of his famous publication, *The Wealth of Nations*. Smith's book provided the spark for my definition: **economics is the science of management of wealth for a nation or a division of a nation.** This statement has a substantial amount of information, so it should be dissected and analyzed in separate pieces.

First and most importantly, economics is a unique and independent science. Many consider it a social science. In this book science is defined as a persistent search for a truly better way to perform an action or understand a condition, process, or thing. Economics is a science concerned with finding better ways to maximize the wealth of a nation or its divisions. To avoid redundancy, please review the analysis of science in the "Introduction" chapter of this book for more information. Economics should be classified as a science for the same reasons finance is.

Second, management is defined as the conducting of various activities for the purpose of meeting specific goals. The goals of economics will be addressed shortly.

Third, this field pertains to the management of wealth. Although I believe many economic academics may agree with my definition of the science of economics, defining wealth is not as easy to form a consensus on. The problems presented for determining wealth are more debatable for economics than for finance, where wealth is defined as the net worth of an individual, a group, or an organization. Net worth is the total assets minus the total liabilities as reflected on the balance sheet. Although we could add more requirements to the definition of wealth, for the sake of simplicity this definition serves as an excellent foundation for finance.

However, many economists could argue economics is too different to fit the above definition of wealth. Many of them consider wealth the annual produce of a nation's land and labor. This definition is certainly important, and does highlight an essential component of economic wealth. However, I have always felt it is incomplete. Using the definition of wealth as applied to finance for economics as well allows for a more extensive definition to include all important aspects of wealth, not just the produce. That is, economic wealth should include at bare minimum an assessment of all of the total assets and all of the total debt of a country. When the total debt is subtracted from the total assets, what is left is the country's net worth.

This amount is as important for a nation as for any individual, group, or organization because it allows a country to know what it is truly worth after all debts are factored in. What little good is gained from knowing the value of the annual produce of a nation's land and labor when the country is technically insolvent? The annual produce is equivalent to a company or an individual's annual income, which is very important, yet only a part of understanding whether or not an individual, a group, an organization, or a nation is truly wealthy. The big picture must also be assessed. This is what wealth takes into account when defined as net worth. Although net worth does have limitations, as listed in the "What Is Finance?" chapter, it is strong enough to serve as a good foundational definition of wealth for both economics and finance.

The last part of the definition of economics pertains to a nation or a division of a nation. This includes any whole nation geographically as big as the United States or as small as Switzerland. Size does not matter as long as the nation functions collectively free from external control by other nations. A limitation may be the ambiguity created by certain scenarios, for example when a country is in political upheaval and becomes divided by civil war. In that situation it may be difficult to pinpoint what area is the nation, as the national boundary lines may be shifting from moment to moment. However, in the normal course of affairs, this explanation of a nation should be sufficient.

The definition of economics also pertains to a separate division of a nation, for example a city or state. This part of the definition was included because many times people are interested in knowing the overall economic health of a specific region, e.g. Philadelphia or Pennsylvania. There may be certain divisions within a nation that economically outperform others. Every economic entity has its own specific budget and economic goals to attend to. Each entity also has its own economic managers in charge of these goals. These economic entities may have different results, similar to two corporations with similar goals and similar initial budgets. This may occur because the performance of economic managers, similar to financial managers, generally differs from one economic entity to the next.

The above definition of economics does not apply to specific agencies or departments within a nation or a division of a nation.

For example, the management of wealth for the Federal Bureau of Investigation or the Food and Drug Administration may fall under the umbrella of finance. These departments function as organizations with specific goals that may be separate from the national economic goals, which will be defined momentarily.

There may be certain scenarios where an organization falls under the umbrella of both finance and economics. For example, any Department of Revenue for a nation or a division of a nation can be classified as an organization and be considered relevant to finance. As an organization this department has needs to fulfill to be able to keep running. It needs to use allocated funds to hire personnel, pay its utility bills, etc. Its goal is to maximize its wealth continuously in order to survive comfortably. However, a Department of Revenue's main function is to collect revenue from taxpayers for the nation. This translates into dual roles: helping to meet the nation's goal of continuously maximizing its wealth in order to survive, and acting as the billing department of a large organization, except here the organization is the nation or a division of it. The Department of Revenue is a special example of a situation where an organization, serving two purposes, can be classified as relevant to both economics and finance depending on which aspect of the department is being assessed.

To conclude, the definition of economics should be understood as the science of managing the wealth of a nation or a division of a nation. In other words, it is the science of conducting various activities for the purpose of meeting specific goals relative to the net worth of a nation or a division of a nation (for example a city or a state). The goals of economics will be the focus of the next chapter.

# CHAPTER 14

# Purposes and Goals of Economics

**The purpose of economics is to continuously seek, analyze, and implement better ways to maximize wealth for a nation or a division of a nation.** Building wealth is a process that never stops. It is very difficult for a nation to become wealthy with the fruits of its people's labor, and even harder to maintain this wealth. This statement illustrates the significance of economics, which is more than learning how to make wealth but how to ensure it is not lost.

A nation's wealth is only as strong as its latest economic policies. A nation could have had a successful economy for centuries, and suddenly its leaders change course and start implementing bad economic policies that lead to misfortune. This scenario is very familiar in history, and is a major reason for the fall of various empires. *All of a nation's hard-earned wealth may be lost in an instant if its leaders neglect to implement intelligent actions learned from economics.*

What are we trying to accomplish by studying economics? There are many goals that ultimately could be condensed to one major goal: **to continuously maximize wealth for a nation or a division of a nation.** Again the word *continuously* is stressed. Maximization of wealth is not something that should be done solely for any random moment in time, for example by Friday, December 31, at 5:00 p.m. EST. To specify one moment in time is to imply that all other moments thereafter are irrelevant. To build wealth for one day and neglect it the next day, year, or decade is nonsensical. Building wealth for a nation or a division of a nation must be an ongoing process with a long-term focus. *Nations that focus their economic goals only on specific moments and keep their goals short-term in nature inevitably regress.*

The major goal of economics is actually a final product of many smaller important goals, or *secondary goals*. Let's explore these now in order to understand the major goal better.

The first secondary goal of economics is to maximize cash inflow. National income is derived mainly from the taxes of taxpaying entities, including individuals and corporations. Nations can meet this goal by increasing tax, or when there are increased sources of revenue for the same tax (for example, if citizens are making more money, there will be more money subject to income tax). The art of economics, however, understands that if a nation taxes its citizens too much their wealth will decrease, potentially resulting in a long-term effect of less income for the nation.

Another secondary economic goal is to maximize surplus, or as we call it in finance, *profits*. This goal is an extension of the first secondary goal, as a surplus is what is left over from revenues after expenses are paid. Another secondary goal is to minimize costs. If the expenses can be reduced to as close to zero, or zero if possible, that would enhance surplus simultaneously.

A fourth secondary goal is to reduce total liabilities. Debt can be helpful in certain circumstances; however, in general, having no debt is preferable. If a nation can have all of its assets in place but make its debt magically disappear then that is a major improvement on its economic position.

A fifth secondary goal of economics is to maximize the nation's assets. Various categories of economic assets can be highly subjective. Some economists argue for inclusion of items ranging from national infrastructure to GDP, but that discussion is beyond the scope of this book. A sixth secondary goal is to avoid bankruptcy. Nations go bankrupt too, and the consequences are more serious than a corporate bankruptcy, as it affects all of its residents.

Before our discussion of economic goals is concluded, we must note that they should not be based on mere survival for any modern nation. In this sense the word *survival* means having just enough income to pay off expenses in order to exist. A goal of mere survival for a nation or a division of a nation would conflict with the interests of the individuals, groups, and organizations that function within that nation. Every individual, group, or organization needs money to live and desires more money (and consequentially more wealth as money is just a part of wealth) than less. If the nation doesn't focus on increasing its wealth, the

THE NECESSITY OF FINANCE

individuals, groups, and organizations within that nation indirectly suffer the consequences.

*A modern nation that chooses not to continuously increase its wealth in both the short and the long term chooses to struggle economically.* A modern nation that chooses not to decrease or increase its wealth, a stagnant nation, chooses to struggle economically as well, as it continuously runs the risk of falling off the edge, into the valleys of wealth minimization. It would be safer for a nation to strive to maximize their wealth instead and increase their odds of avoiding an economic struggle. **Economic lessons throughout the ages have taught us that a nation that struggles economically translates to individuals, groups, and organizations of the nation struggling in every aspect of life.**

# CHAPTER 15

# Economic Conclusions

The definition, purpose, and goals of economics proposed in this book are generally consistent with the various types of economic systems used. To demonstrate this, let's first look at a brief overview of the types of governments and economic systems.

The types of governments enforced within a nation are different from its economic systems, and the types must be differentiated. Types of governments include but are not limited to monarchies, aristocracies, dictatorships, democracies, republics, and democratic republics. Each type demonstrates the way a nation is ruled. In a monarchy, a nation is ruled by a king or queen. In an aristocracy, a nation is ruled by a wealthy minority. In a dictatorship, a nation is ruled by one person or a small group of people. In a democracy, a nation is ruled by the people who live in it. This is very difficult to enact in larger nations, thus the government converts to a republic, where it is ruled by elected representatives of the people. Finally a democratic republic is usually a misnomer, and can take on different forms.

The definition, purpose, and goals of economics are consistent with any of the government types above. Although world peace is a desirable outcome for many, that does not change the governmental behavior of nations. Regardless if a nation is organized as a monarchy or a republic, modern governments strive to create stronger nations, to rival competitor nations. They do this by managing their wealth in order to increase economic prosperity. If a country is wealthy it can afford to create better technological weapons, strengthen its security, and pay for a standing army, one of the best military groups that can be created. A standing army allows for full-time soldiers dedicated to learning how to protect the nation. Thus any king or queen, dictator (if he understands and cares about what is best for the nation in the long run), and especially any people's republic or form of one will strive for creating a wealthier nation, at least for the sole reason of having a stronger nation. If the nation is not strong, any rival nation can conquer it and easily alter its government and form. *Thus a major goal of any government of a nation is also a goal of the nation: to continuously maximize the wealth of the nation. If the goal is to continuously minimize the wealth of the nation there will not be enough to support needed military protection, and the government risks losing its nation to invaders.*

The economic systems enforced within a nation include, but are not limited to laissez faire, totalitarianism, socialism, communism, monetarism, and Keynesian. These systems are mainly organized based on the degree of government control that is allowed, with laissez faire and totalitarian systems on extreme opposite sides. Laissez faire, sometimes called capitalism, is considered a purely free-market economic system. That is, the economic system is free from government intervention in all aspects except for the government's basic functions. This is completely the opposite of totalitarianism, where the government controls every aspect of the economic system.

Socialism is characterized by social ownership of the wealth of the nation. This system calls for more government intervention, but not as much as a totalitarian economic system does. Socialism eventually led to the idea of communism as created by Karl Marx. Pure communism, as distinguished from what the idea eventually became, called for the abolishment of property so people could be equal.

Monetarism is basically a form of laissez faire created by Milton Friedman where government is mainly only allowed to control the money supply in targeted amounts. The Keynesian economic system, also called macroeconomics, allows the government to have a significant influence on the economic system through the use of various monetary and fiscal policies while simultaneously allowing the free market to exist.

Many of these economic systems are arguably consistent with the purpose and goals of economics. That is, many of the systems and their policies are put in place in order to assist a nation in meeting the major goal of maximizing its wealth. For example, this goal is generally true for many of the free-market forms of economic systems, which believe if individuals are concerned for their own interests, it has a bettering effect on the whole economy. This is the result of the idea that everyone knows his or her own financial situation better than anyone else does. It is also consistent with the goal of finance in which an individual, a group, or an organization continuously strives to maximize its own wealth. Consequently, the belief is that the wealth of nations is maximized when an individual, a group, or an organization seeks to maximize its wealth.

Nevertheless, some other economic policies appear inconsistent with the purpose and goals of economics. For example, the Keynesian policy, which promotes a nation to spend its money to boost its economy. Some economists subscribe to the belief that spending a nation's wealth will maximize its wealth; others argue it does not. Admittedly the purpose and goal of economics discussed in this book may stir some debate. However, the definition of economics appears very consistent with all of the economic policies listed above. **Regardless of whether or not any economic policy has positive or negative effects on a nation, or for whatever reason does not have a goal to continuously maximize wealth, the polices still fall under the umbrella of economics as defined in this book, which is the science of managing wealth for a nation or a division of a nation.**

Finally, the newly stated definition, purpose, and goals are generally consistent with the various fields of economics, which covers topics all across the board, including inflation, unemployment, population control, union wages, health insurance, taxation, national debt, tariffs, trade embargos, government price fixing, monetary and fiscal policy, imports and exports, minimum wages, and rent control. There are so many different fields of economics that our definition will help to finally allow these categories to be well organized and have some direction. That is, viewing these subjects from the perspective that they are all part of a science dealing with managing the wealth of a nation or a division of a nation helps us to understand each subject's direction. It shouldn't matter whether an economist is discussing inflation or embargoes. All of the topics are concerned with the bigger picture of managing the wealth of the nation.

Many of these different fields and topics should also be concerned with the purpose and goal of economics. Nations should strive to manage and maximize their wealth. It's more sensible than the alternative, to minimize it. This is so for dealing with different types of governments. If a nation has a foolish goal of minimizing wealth and succeeds then it chooses to let its people to struggle and increases the probability of foreign conquest. If economists adopt this approach to economics, the field may find its topics more organized, sensible, and consistent, which may help accelerate further improvements in the science.

# CHAPTER 16

# The Relationship between Finance and Economics

## A Special Synergy

We have fully analyzed the definition, purpose, and goals of finance and economics. Now it is time to assess the relationship between the two sciences. Although there are many aspects of the two that appear interrelated, they can mainly be divided based on the entity on which the science focuses. In finance, the science of the management of wealth is focused on an individual, a group, or an organization. In economics, the science of the management of wealth is focused on a nation or a division of a nation.

The common ground between the two sciences is that they both concentrate on the management of wealth. In all its forms, including cash, wealth must be managed so as to be continuously maximized for its owning entity.

Seeing this distinction, one may wonder why we don't classify finance and economics together, as they both focus on wealth management. We could call the new field the science of wealth management, and any entity that has anything to do with the subject would be a part of the umbrella science. Under that philosophy it would also make sense to lump together biology, physics, and chemistry, as they all have something to do with the science of life but from different perspectives.

Economics and finance must be distinguished for the same reason. Even though they both focus on wealth management, they view the subject from different perspectives that are so different the concepts within each science make more sense when analyzed isolated from the other science. For example, inflation planning means something completely different for the focused entities of finance compared to the focused entities of economics. Individuals, groups, and organizations cannot control inflation but must deal with it to meet their goals of continuously maximizing their wealth. On the other hand, a nation has a significantly high probability of controlling inflation as it has the ability to influence the printing of money. Thus, finance and economics have many similarities in structure but not in focus.

Managing the wealth of a nation encompasses significantly different variables than managing the wealth of an individual, a group, or an organization. Although the fundamental ideas are mostly the same, there are so many differences in the needs of the two focused entity groups it is more sensible to have two separate sciences. Economics needs to focus on the bigger picture. Managing the wealth of nations encompasses incorporating bigger variables that may be irrelevant for an individual, a group, or an organization. For example, searching for better ways to deal with welfare issues so that there is a proper balance between happy citizens and a wealthy nation is a task more fit for economics. Of course a nation can abolish welfare; many economists would view this action as maximizing the wealth of a nation because they consider it a wasteful program. Other economists argue that welfare does maximize the wealth of a nation because it helps those who need some assistance to maximize their individual wealth. This help in turn may eventually lead to more-productive citizens and more wealth for the nation. This example illustrates two arguments for improving the wealth of a nation as it appears through the lens of an economist.

The economist is trained to look at all of the unique scenarios that arise for national wealth management but do not occur for the entities of which the nation is comprised. To demonstrate let's take a look at the same situation from the individual perspective. Generally, the issue of welfare will only be directly applicable to individuals who stand to gain or lose from the welfare program. If the program is removed, an individual who depends on that money to live, Individual A, will need to find another source of income. Thus this situation has immediately affected the way Individual A needs to manage his wealth. In order to maximize it, Individual A will need to find a job or other assistance from another direction.

Individual B, on the other hand, has a steady job and does not depend on welfare, nor does anyone in her family. The removal of welfare does not have any direct effect on Individual B.

Nevertheless, a welfare program does cost money that will indirectly affect most taxpayers, including Individual B, as it must be paid for by a tax on income. Thus, although the program may affect all financial entities indirectly, as shown above, it may not affect them all directly. This scenario illustrates that issues that may directly affect the way a nation maximizes its wealth may or may not directly affect the way the individuals, groups, and organizations that comprise a nation maximizes their wealth.

There is another way to view the relationship between the two subjects. Economics focuses on directly maximizing the wealth of the bigger unit, the nation, while its policies may have indirect effects on the wealth of its comprising smaller units. Contrarily, finance focuses on directly maximizing the wealth of the smaller units called *financial entities*, the individuals, groups, and organizations, while its decisions may have indirect effects on the wealth of the larger unit, the nation.

The whole of anything is the sum of its parts. The same can be said about the goals of finance and economics. If a nation strives to continuously maximize its wealth and succeeds, this may result in the nation's average individual, group, or organization obtaining increased wealth. I use the word *average* because when dealing with people there will always be unique situations that will not allow all to obtain increased wealth (for example, incompetency, gambling problems, etc.). In other words, if a nation is wealthy then that may generally equate to the average person, group, or organization of a nation being wealthy.

The opposite is also true. If the average individual, group, or organization strives to continuously maximize its wealth and succeeds, this may result in the nation they are a part of obtaining increased wealth. In other words, if the average person, group, or organization of a nation is wealthy then that may generally equate to a wealthy nation.

Communism, specifically as implemented in the former USSR, is proof of these two statements. Communism was not successful, as it had appeared to be for many decades. When the Berlin Wall fell, the truth was revealed. The USSR was not as wealthy as its leaders portrayed to the world because its average person was not wealthy. Actually it was revealed that its average citizen was struggling for essential needs like food and water. If the USSR's economic policies had been successful, in the long run it might have had increased wealth for its average citizen and consequently been a wealthier nation. Viewing the situation from the other way around produces the same effect: if the economic policies of the USSR had produced an ideal climate where average individuals, groups, or organizations could have created wealth then the nation may also have obtained increased wealth in the long run, assuming its liabilities were in check.

An argument against the above conclusions is a scenario where the people appear mainly wealthy, but the nation is increasingly in debt and losing wealth. To address this problem, the nation prints more money, to make the debt worthless. This argument is based on perception. The people perceive they are getting wealthier because many of the average individuals, groups, and organizations appear to be getting wealthier. This may be the result of a short-term effect that hasn't registered in the big picture yet.

Realistically, if a nation's debt is increasing and being paid by printing more money, the net effect is a decrease in wealth for all of its parts because individuals, groups, and organizations will need more money to buy the same amount of goods as before. Thus this argument, when thought through, does not conflict with the above statement. In this scenario a nation is actually getting poorer, and so are its people.

Let's look at one more counterargument to this subject. Nations throughout history have been portrayed as wealthy though the majority of their people were not wealthy. In many cases this was due to the amount of slaves, or people living in a state similar to slavery, the nation held. A nation, for our purposes, is a collection of its people, and that includes people who are considered slaves. Thus, a perceived wealthy nation that had a majority of poor slaves or people living in a state similar to slavery was not a truly wealthy nation. It may have had some wealth, but it was not maximizing its wealth until it demonstrated consideration for the needs of all its individuals. For what is a nation without including its entire people?

In this scenario, the goal of economics could only be accomplished by eliminating slavery. Thus those nations that had wealth really only demonstrated that they were striving to maximize the wealth of a small minority of people and not the average individual's wealth. *Consider the slave nation's lost opportunity of potential wealth if it allowed its entire people the liberty to maximize their wealth. It's not hard to take this one step further and envision ancient nations already at the state of current civilization many years ahead of time.*

We can now conclude that although they are two different sciences, there is a special synergy between finance and economics. Together both are necessary sciences dealing with issues that affect every aspect of modern human life. These sciences should be studied separately for focus on a specific discipline. However, both may be studied together by economists and financialists for a complete, holistic picture of the different perspectives pertaining to wealth management.

## The Idea of Finance Was Always There

I have spent much time contemplating why finance did not emerge first as a formal modern science instead of economics. One answer to this riddle can be found in history. The need to manage wealth was initially considered, in a basic form, by ancient civilizations like the ancient Egyptians, Greeks, and Romans. However, considering that those nations were generally controlled by a wealthy minority, we can see how economics and finance were probably perceived as almost one and the same. Maybe, to these ancient nations, the wealthy minority that happened to rule the nation only contemplated maximizing their own wealth. The wealth of the people, as in all members of the nation, was probably not entirely factored in. Thus to manage the wealth of the wealthy minority was perceived as the same as managing the wealth of the nation.

Many years later, around the time of the American and French Revolutions, for the first time very large groups of people started demanding to be respected as equal members of society, with rights to maximize their own wealth. Ironically this was around the time of *The Wealth of Nations*. The average member of society now wanted a piece of the pie; he wanted an opportunity to maximize his own wealth. In order to do that, he needed to reside in a nation with the proper type of government, one that promoted freedom for its citizens.

Adam Smith's *The Wealth of Nations* was the spark that ignited the flame. His book reflected on the path a nation could take to maximize its wealth. This was the first time a book of this magnitude reflected on serious national and individual issues of wealth management. The books published after *The Wealth of Nations* set the direction for the eventual creation of a science called economics as they followed Smith's argument only as it applied to nations. Although individual wealth management was relevant at the time, as in the time of the ancients, there was still such a minority of wealthy people in the world that a science pertaining to the wealth of nations may have been more relevant for that period.

In the twentieth century, the demographics of wealth shifted like at no other time in history. For the first time, a very large population of selected nations was considered wealthy. This may have been the catalyst for the birth of modern finance. **The idea of finance was always there, but was never quite prepared for analysis until recently. Finance may have been formalized much sooner, but it was missing the right political and economic environments for the wealthiest nations, like what has occurred in the past two centuries, to create more wealthy individuals, groups, and organizations so the need for the science could be truly realized.** This brings us to the present. Although finance has been taught at universities for several decades now, the idea of finance as a completely separate science, finally distinguished from the shadows of economics, has come.

# CHAPTER 17

# Financial Economics and Economic Finance

Given the previous chapters' analysis of finance and economics, we may conclude the term *financial economics* is a misnomer, but that depends on how the phrase is used. I don't want to confuse you; the message should still be clear that finance is not economics, and economics is not finance. Thus, it is incorrect to refer to finance as discussed in this book as financial economics.

However, there may be a place for such a specialty field in economics. This specialization would need economists who are interested in learning about the science of managing the wealth of an individual, a group, or an organization in order to help meet the goal of continuously maximizing the wealth of a nation or a division of one. In other words, people who study financial economics would do it for the reason of meeting the goal of economics and not finance. By studying how financial entities continuously maximize wealth, economists striving to maximize the wealth of a nation may be able to gain better insight.

To be clear, if a person is a financial economist he is still an economist. If a person focuses on finance he is a financialist. This clarification highlights the problems associated with the origins of modern finance. Its founders were mostly economists who considered themselves financial economists. This term would only be applicable if their focus had been ultimately on maximizing the wealth of a nation or a division of a nation. It was not.

The founders of modern finance were focused on concepts mostly applied to maximizing the wealth of individuals, groups, or organizations. For example, Harry Markowitz's portfolio selection dealt with the relationship between risk and return in the portfolios of financial entities, not the portfolios of nations. I am not trying to discredit anyone or anything published in this book. I am simply noting it is necessary to distinguish the terms used in order to give full credibility to the science of finance.

This analysis may not be complete without an exploration of the reverse situation: a new specialty called *economic finance*. This new, as-yet uncreated field, would need financialists interested in learning about the science of managing the wealth of a nation or a division of one in order to help meet the goal of continuously maximizing the wealth of individuals, groups, or organizations. In other words people would study economic finance for the reason of meeting the goal of finance, not economics. By studying how economic entities continuously maximize wealth, a financialist may be able to find better ways to maximize the wealth of an individual, a group, or an organization. To be clear, if you are an economic financialist then you are still a financialist.

# CHAPTER 18

# Types of Finance

## Overview

Many subjects are interrelated with finance and are currently taught as parts of finance programs. These subjects include but are not limited to marketing, human resource management, accounting, statistics, management, investing, business law, risk management, insurance, behavioral finance, personal finance, corporate finance, public finance, and, of course, economics. Many of these subjects also go by different names or branches of the main subject. For example, corporate finance is sometimes referred to as managerial finance or finance for decision making. Some of these subjects are entirely different sciences, for example economics.

So many subjects have been lumped together with finance since the subject started to appear in universities, it is very overwhelming for students to understand the main focus of the science. The basic definition, purpose, and goals of finance need to be universally understood in order to organize all of these subjects. New financial fields appear at least every decade, pushing us further from an opportunity for clarification of the science. The inevitably result for finance could be similar to the process endured by economics: about 250 years without a true, clear understanding of the science.

How much longer can finance go on in its current form, without students knowing how each related subject fits within the big picture? To address this issue, I have organized finance into two major categories: personal finance, and group and organizational finance. These two groups are consistent with the definition, purpose, and goals of finance as stated in this book. We will now explore each one of these categories.

## Personal Finance

**Personal finance is the science of managing the wealth of an individual or a family.** Although a family is considered a group of individuals, it should be the major exception to be included in personal finance. All other groups, from a local soccer team to a chess club, should be included in group and organizational finance.

The word *group* is used loosely in this book. The major difference between groups and organizations is the size of the entity and the general level of formality. In general, the larger and more formal entities will be considered organizations. As *groups* can be an ambiguous term, although it has worked well for the analysis of finance up until this point, it is not practical to have a specific category for groups. It is much easier to bridge the connection as presented here.

**The purpose of personal finance is to continuously seek, analyze, and implement better ways to maximize wealth for an individual or a family. The major goal of personal finance is to continuously maximize wealth for an individual or a family.** Personal finance is a subject everyone should study regardless of his or her specialization or occupation. All individuals need to understand how to maximize their wealth as a condition of their survival. This is especially applicable if the individuals have a family of others to support.

Personal finance covers various subjects that apply uniquely to individuals and families, thus, which is why it should be distinguished from group and organizational finance. For example, personal finance can include, but is not limited to, education planning, health-care planning, individual tax planning, planning for parenthood, retirement, disability and long-term care insurance, and estate planning. These are all issues that need to be addressed specifically as they apply to individuals and families. Let's take a closer look at why.

Education planning generally involves planning for college, as it is very expensive for the average citizen, and the education industry has one of the highest inflation rates. Education planning is unique to an individual as it relates to managing the individual's or family's wealth. A group or organization may only be concerned with education planning if it is relevant to their goals. Even if an individual is part of a group that provides assistance with educational planning, it is the individual who ultimately needs to make the right choices in order to maximize his or her wealth. In short, groups and organizations have their own financial goals to meet, which are separate from the financial goals at the personal level.

Retirement planning is another example of a subject that can uniquely apply to individuals and families. Individuals are responsible for ensuring they have enough saved for retirement, not a group or organization. For example, companies may offer pensions, 401(k)s, and other retirement plans, but that does not guarantee that the vested amount will be enough to meet the needs of their individual employees at their planned retirement dates. The individuals need to do the soul searching to forecast what their specific needs will be in a certain amount of years considering inflation and other factors. The individuals know their own needs and goals best.

Personal finance also deals with situations like how to prepare financially for parenthood or for purchasing a home. These are unique issues, and there are various approaches to them. Only a specialized science can be appropriate for finding truly better ways to maximize one's wealth based off those particular situations. Some common parenting issues include education funding; funding for future weddings or a child's first home; initial costs of early parenthood; and learning better ways to teach one's children about finance. Some common home buying issues include one's options to rent or buy a home; how big the home should be; what the various costs of buying a home are; secondary home purchases; and the location of property.

Personal finance also addresses one of the biggest financial issues for individuals currently residing in the United States: health care. As one of the biggest costs for the average American, it is very important for an individual or family who is trying to meet their financial goals to incorporate a plan to deal with health care. This may include finding an employer that offers benefits, selecting individual health care plans, or even utilizing welfare.

Personal finance is also concerned with finding optimal ways to reduce income tax. If one can legally lower or avoid income tax then he has essentially contributed to his financial goal of maximizing wealth. Lowering taxes translates to increasing wealth because it allows one to retain money that otherwise would have been paid out.

Personal finance is also concerned with various types of necessary insurance, such as disability insurance. There is a risk that the head of a household may become disabled. If this occurs without proper protection, a family can be devastated until that person can return to work. Disability insurance is a tool to address this situation. There are many different options available and concepts that should be understood before making any financial commitment.

Long-term care planning is another important topic covered by personal finance. If an individual needs assistance with living as he gets older, there should be a plan in place to deal with the unexpected. Some people may maintain their wits until their death, but that is not always the case. Long-term planning insurance can be an effective tool, amongst others, to assist an individual if the need for elderly care ever occurs.

Estate planning is another subject covered in personal finance. Upon the death of an individual, his or her financial situation can be complex and overwhelming for the executors in charge of managing the process. There are also many taxes to consider, and complex situations that can arise without proper planning. Personal finance can provide many tools for individuals to utilize in conjunction with advice from their attorneys on how to maximize the wealth that will be passed to their beneficiaries.

To summarize, personal finance is a category of finance that pertains to wealth management for an individual or a family. Personal finance can benefit individuals and families who are interested in maximizing their wealth and improving their chances of comfortable survival in our modern civilization.

## Group and Organizational Finance

**Group and organizational finance is the science of managing wealth for a group or an organization.** Although a family is considered a group of individuals, it should be excluded from this category. **The purpose of group and organizational finance is to continuously seek, analyze, and implement better ways to maximize wealth for a group or an organization. The major goal is to continuously maximize wealth for a group or an organization.**

The category of group and organizational finance was created because it can include a wide variety of specific financial subjects in order to better organize finance as a whole. This new category includes, but is not limited to, the following subjects only when they pertain to groups and organizations: corporate finance, investments, entrepreneurial finance, nonprofit financial management, managerial finance, public finance, management, human resources, marketing, and the newly introduced economic finance (see chapter seventeen, "Financial Economics and Economic Finance").

Corporate finance is the science of managing wealth for a corporation. Generally this subject is focused on private as well as publicly listed corporations. The term *going public* refers to the process of selling shares of stocks to investors on a public stock exchange in exchange for ownership of the company. Almost anyone from the general public can purchase the shares of public corporations. Corporate finance, although very important, only focuses on a segment of organizations, corporations. Thus, by itself, this subject does not cover enough range to be considered an entire category.

Nonprofit financial management is the science of managing wealth for nonprofit organizations, which generally include any legally organized organization that has a goal to use its profits to fund a specific cause to benefit society, for example fighting poverty in underdeveloped countries, or a specific disease. The idea is that the company's profits are not intended for the benefit of the owners.

Public finance is the science of managing wealth for public organizations. It's a subject that borders economics as defined in this book. To recall, economics may not apply to specific agencies or departments within a nation or a division of a nation. Public finance is more appropriate for departments that function as organizations with specific goals that may be separate from the national economic goals. For example, the management of wealth for the Federal Bureau of Investigation or the Food and Drug Administration may fall under the umbrella of public finance.

Managerial finance (sometimes called financial management) is a very loosely defined subject at many universities. All finance specialties in this book pertain to the management of wealth. Thus the question becomes: whose wealth is being managed? Managerial finance is not extensive enough to be considered a major category of finance because it generally does not include analyses of wealth management for nonprofit and public organizations. Most courses in managerial finance focus on how it relates to businesses, but it mainly focuses on large corporations and very little on smaller businesses. Thus this subject would be best consolidated based on who is the focus of the wealth management. If it's corporations then the subject should be properly titled *corporate finance*. If the focus is on managing wealth for small businesses then the subject should be properly titled *small business finance*.

If you believe that humans can be considered assets then human resources (HR) and general management can be placed within the new category of group and organizational finance. Because these subjects deal with the management of human assets, a component of wealth, they can be considered part of finance. Admittedly this is a radical view of HR and management, but it is sensible framed within our analysis.

Human resources pertains to the hiring and firing of employees for a group or organization. Management pertains to educating the manager, whose job is to conduct various activities for the purpose of meeting specific goals. Both subjects deal with managing human assets, from hiring or firing employees to instructing managers of other assets. As such HR and management's ultimate goal is parallel to the goal of group and organization finance: to continuously maximize wealth for a group or an organization.

Marketing, in essence, focuses on building strong relationships with various members of society, especially customers and potential customers, for groups or organizations in order to continuously maximize their wealth. In other words, because this subject deals with the management of wealth, specifically building wealth, marketing can be considered a part of finance. As such its ultimate goal is parallel to the goal of group and organization finance: to continuously maximize wealth for a group or an organization.

The subjects noted above, and others, may also be organized as either personal finance or group and organizational finance depending on who is the focus of wealth management. For example, behavioral finance includes the study of psychological reasons for the behavior of the stock market. This field can be incorporated under personal finance or group and organizational finance depending on whether the focus is on an individual, a family, a group, or an organization. For example, if the study of the concepts of behavioral finance will assist in continuously maximizing the wealth of an individual or a family then it would be best categorized under personal finance.

Investments (sometimes called investing) is another example of a subject that may be organized under either of the major finance categories depending on who is the focus of wealth management.

The goal of investments (or investing) is the same as finance: to maximize wealth for a specific financial entity. However, the subject of investments is often confused with the whole science of finance. In reality investing and investments, although very important, are only part of the big picture. Officially all investments fit only on the asset side of the balance sheet; they are not liabilities.

With that said, there are other aspects of finance that need to be considered in addition to investments, such as hoarded cash, debt, and equity. Learning about investments or how to invest should be understood as a subcomponent of finance and not the entire science. This subject can be attributed to personal finance or group and organizational finance depending on whose wealth should be maximized. In other words, if the study of the subject of investments will assist in continuously maximizing wealth for an individual or a family, it would be best categorized under personal finance. If it will assist in continuously maximizing wealth for a group or an organization, it would be best categorized under group and organizational finance.

Entrepreneurial finance is a newer subject being taught in universities. This subject appears very loosely defined, basically is directed at finance as it applies to entrepreneurs. An entrepreneur is an individual who starts and manages his or her own business. Thus, entrepreneurial finance is about the science of managing wealth for an entrepreneurial business. If the business has only one entrepreneur, the subject should be organized under personal finance. If there are two or more entrepreneurs starting a business, it should be organized under group and organizational finance. This field seems promising, but currently there appears to be too much overlap and little direction.

Accounting, one of the oldest subjects in human civilization, also fits into this newer organizational model. Originally called bookkeeping, it can be described as a systematic recording and administration of financial data for an individual, a group, or an organization. Accounting will be categorized here as a sub-science of finance because it is consistent with the definition, purpose, and goals of finance. This makes more sense when you consider why financial data is recorded. Sometimes an entity has to do it, for example in a public corporation that is required to submit financial statements to the public. Why do they have to? And what are they afraid of if they don't? In this case they have to because they don't want to risk minimizing their wealth through penalties that regulators can impose on them. Actually, in all aspects of accounting, financial data is recorded and adminis-tered to assist with financial goals. Recording data helps to mea-sure progress toward the wealth-maximizing goal of finance. In other words, accounting is an essential subject that also has a main goal of continuously maximizing wealth for an individual, a group, or an organization.

*Without accounting or its tools, finance would be extremely disorganized and random. All assets and liabilities would exist only in memory. However, without financial data, accounting would be nonexistent.* There is no need to record financial data if all forms of assets and liabilities are absent.

It's thought that accounting first began in ancient Mesopotamia, when people needed to record the development of crops and herds. Considering that crops and herds were consid-ered assets in ancient times, accounting would have been created as a direct outcome of the purpose of finance: to continuously seek, analyze, and implement better ways to maximize wealth for an individual, a group, or an organization. Thus, accounting is a result of finding a better way to maximize wealth.

Accounting also can be organized as either personal finance or group and organizational finance depending on who is the focus of wealth management. If the financial data recorded is relevant to an individual or family then the subject can be included under personal finance. If it's relevant to a group or organization then the subject can be placed under group and organizational finance.

In summary, the categories of personal finance and group and organizational finance have been created to form a better organizational structure for the various financially related subjects. These categories are consistent with the definition, purpose, and goals of finance. Although some of the subjects may appear inconsistent at first, when the whole of the argument is thought through, the organizational scheme should prove to be beneficial. HR, management, marketing, and accounting are subjects that have danced around business schools for many years without guidance as proper sciences. However, when their bottom line goal, wealth maximization for various entities is considered, these subjects can be organized under the realm of finance.

Academics and practitioners in these fields do not need to be offended or alarmed by the above proposal. If anything strength is found in numbers. By following the organizational pattern, these subjects can be united under one umbrella science. The long-term effect of this could be a stronger, more unified method to approaching these sciences, more respect for all of these subjects, and more validity for the science of finance and all of its existing subsciences.

# CHAPTER 19

# Finance and Business

The subject of business and its relationship to finance can best be understood by starting with a practical definition. **A *business* is an entity formed by an individual, a group, or an organization to sell goods and services in order to maximize profits and eventually distribute a part or all of them to the owners.**

First, a business is an entity that consists of a unit of one or more people with the same goals. This entity should function as one. Second, a business must be formed by an individual, a group, or an organization. Thus, a business must be created by something as opposed to just magically appearing for some unexplained reason. Also, unlike a human who can only be created when a partnership is made between two individuals, a business entity can be created by one or more individuals. For example, in the case of a sole proprietorship (this will be discussed momentarily) the business is created by one individual.

Third, the main distinguishing function of a business is to sell goods or services. Therefore, the science of sales is an extremely important part of business. A business can sell goods, services, or both as the choice is up to the owners, but they must sell something to be called a business.

In terms of selling goods, a business may buy them first from another business, as in the case of wholesalers and retailers. Alternatively the owners or their employees may make the goods themselves (possibly from raw materials). With either format, in the end, if a business owner chooses to sell goods, the business must have something for sale to present to potential buyers. The buyers generally are not concerned with the various stages of the product's assembly (although this information may be very helpful). Instead, they are mostly concerned with the final product offered and its price.

A business may choose to sell services instead of products. Services are intangible products that require actions to be performed. Examples of people involved in service-oriented businesses include surgeons, beauticians, and mail carriers. A business can also sell both products and services, for example a restaurant. It can provide goods, or the food it prepares. As far as services, if you dine in then you may have to pay a service charge for being served by a waiter or waitress. In some cases the charge may not be required formally, but informally through recommended tips.

A business is created to maximize profits from the sale of goods or services. Profits are defined as the result of income minus expenses and taxes. Profits, although just a part of wealth, is the motivating force that brings people together to unite and create businesses. Of course, like all financial entities, businesses should also focus on maximizing total wealth and not just profits.

Finally, the owners that form a business have the intention of taking a distribution of the profits one day, whether it is next month or in an indefinite time in the future. There is a common misconception that not all businesses are for profit. In the context of the above definition, it should be clear that all businesses should have a profit motive. If an entity does not have a profit motive then it will be better classified as something else, such as a traditional individual, group, or organization. In addition, business owners must have the intention of keeping a part or all of the profits at some point in the future. This is the major difference between a business and a nonprofit organization.

A nonprofit organization is sometimes called a nonprofit *business*. Technically, this is not correct for several reasons. As noted above, it would be more proper to call it an *organization* as it is not a business. Second, as will be explained, these organizations have profits, but they are not for the owners to keep. A nonprofit (or charitable) organization, although very similar to a business, is not a business. **A nonprofit organization is an entity formed by an individual, a group, or an organization to sell goods and services in order to maximize profits and eventually distribute a part or all of them to a specific cause.**

You may be confused by the inclusion of the word *profits* in this definition. A nonprofit organization should function in many regards like a business. It may have income, expenses, profits, losses, assets, and liabilities just like any financial entity.

A nonprofit organization is different from a business mainly because the profits are directed to a cause instead of to the owners, for example, to curing a specific disease.

A nonprofit must generate income from selling goods and services. However, the types of goods and services it sells may not directly benefit the buyer. In this case, the buyer is said to have made a donation. However, with deep reflection one can see that a donation is really a sale of a good or service for the direct benefit of someone other than the buyer; the buyer gains an indirect benefit in the form of the pleasure of giving. For example consider a hypothetical nonprofit organization called Charity ABCD that was started to help fight poverty in Country Z. If people donate to Charity ABCD's cause then essentially they are indirectly buying food and services from Charity ABCD to give to affected poor people in Country Z. Indirectly the donators are also receiving the pleasure of giving. Some may even argue that this indirect feeling is actually a direct benefit for the buyer, similar to how one pays for the service of a chiropractor or massage therapist to make him or her feel good. Thus donators are really buying an opportunity to be altruistic and receive the feelings that go along with it.

There are many types of businesses that can be setup, including sole proprietorships, partnerships, limited liability companies (LLCs), limited liability partnership (LLPs), S corporations, and the traditional C corporations. Each of these types may be formed by a financial entity based on its needs.

When choosing a business type, it is important for the financial entity to consider its whole situation, including what its monetary and nonmonetary goals are now and in the future.

A financial entity must also consider: how much control it would like to have over the company; how much effort it would like to exert to create and administer the business; the maximum liability of the owner or owners; taxes; the ease of obtaining funding; etc. For example, a sole proprietorship is a business formed by one individual who wants to take on all risks, answers only to the customer, has unlimited profit potential, and wants the business to stop when he or she dies. Although the owner is a living being, when a sole proprietor acts in accordance with the above definition of a business then he or she is acting as a business. As soon as he or she stops selling goods or services or performing any functions that are aimed at profit maximization, he or she reverts back to a non-business state. *The old proverb "it's nothing personal, it's just business" highlights the distinction between the two different conscious levels on which a financial entity may coexist: personal and business.* However, there are certainly gray areas. There are many instances when it is hard to tell whether a person is in a normal or a business state of mind.

It is important to clarify the difference between a business and an investment. An *investment* is an asset as defined in this book. A business is a whole unit functioning as one entity. A business can own an investment, which would be classified as an asset on its balance sheet. The investment the business owns can be separate from its regular business that focuses on profit maximization for the goods and services it sells. For example, an airline business may own a large supply of gold and precious metals.

In addition, a business can invest in another business. A business in isolation functions as a whole unit, but it can be an investment asset of another business. For example Company A, which sells Product A, can invest in 10 percent of the stock of Company B, which sells Product B. Company A's main business has not change: it still sells Product A. However, it has increased its stock assets by investing in Company B.

The terms *businessperson, businessman,* and *businesswoman* should be used to describe any person who owns or works for an entity formed by an individual, a group, or an organization to sell goods and services in order to maximize profits and eventually distribute a part or all of it to the owners. There are also different degrees of these individuals. For example, one can be referred to as a good businessperson or a bad businessperson depending on their track record of conducting business.

Naturally, the subject of business should be about understanding various aspects of managing a business. Since business is such a broad category, the term is used too loosely in many situations. There are many university programs and subjects that are classified as business, but with further analysis it makes more sense to classify them as subsciences of finance. **To be clear, all business subjects are a part of finance.** In particular this includes the science of sales, which instructs students on better ways to sell products and services. Selling anything translates ultimately to making money and wealth maximization, the central focal point of finance.

Finance as defined in this book focuses on wealth maximization for various financial entities, that is, for individuals, groups, or organizations, which may or may not be functioning as businesses. Businesses focus mainly on profit maximization, which is only a component of wealth. True business courses must teach the better ways of managing wealth that are learned from the more comprehensive science of finance. In this way students can learn how to maximize all of the wealth of a business, including profits.

With business organized as a subscience of finance, there may be changes in university course coding and program structures. For example, the masters in business administration (MBA), a common degree program, may be viewed in a different perspective. The MBA is a master's degree in business, which is essentially a subscience of finance. This viewpoint may require more business programs to include other types of other finance classes. Also this new perspective would eliminate any status of a concentration or minor in finance. It would become the major, and business could be the minor.

To be consistent with the two categories of finance mentioned before, business can be organized as either personal finance or group and organizational finance depending on who is the focus of wealth management. For example, if the business in question is a sole proprietorship then it will fit under the personal finance category. If it is a corporation then it will fit under the group and organizational finance category. These new arrangements for business courses are consistent with the definition, purpose, and goals of finance as stated in this book.

Business courses have long been wandering without proper direction and an official science to call home. Finally, with business finding a home under the science of finance, it could have all of the benefits mentioned before about the organization of the other finance-related subjects. That is, the long-term effect of this could be a stronger, more unified method of approaching business, more respect for all business subjects, and more validity for the science of finance and all of the existing subsciences.

# CHAPTER 20

# The Necessity of Financial Planning

## The Holistic Approach to Financial Planning

More proof of the necessity of finance occurred in the mid-1960s, when financial planners first appeared. For the first time in history, the common people had a serious need for this service, probably due to the exponential growth of wealth for individuals, groups, and organizations in America and the economic policies at the time. Beginning in the 1970s, the financial planning industry became more structured, and various certifications and designations were created to better qualify practitioners in the field. These actions demonstrated the growing demand for the development of the science of finance.

Financial planning is an often-confused term. Although regulators have their own definition of financial planning, the following discussion is based on the term from an academic standpoint only. To understand financial planning, first we must make distinctions between four groups of people: financial managers, financial consultants, financial advisors, and financial planners. To review, a financial manager is anyone who manages wealth for an individual, a group, or an organization. *Managing* will be defined as conducting various activities for the purpose of meeting specific goals. Thus, a *financial manager* is a comprehensive term that includes conducting a variety of activities in order to maximize the wealth of the above entities. The financial manager must have every activity focused on this end goal.

To make this discussion easy, the remaining three groups of people will all be considered the same as the financial manager noted above. That is, financial managers, financial consultants, financial advisors, and financial planners will be considered one and the same when viewed from a holistic perspective. This may appear strange at first, but a closer examination of their expected roles will reveal the truth.

A financial manager is involved with activities such as planning and giving advice. Considering that a consultant is a person who gives advice, a financial consultant and financial advisor are terms that essentially mean the same thing. Anyone who consults or gives financial advice to another and truly wants to maximize the other person's wealth will need to be a part of the wealth-management process. To give advice only on one specific part of an entity's financial picture, for example a stock, without assessing the holistic picture may do more harm than good.

Let's suppose a customer asks a waitress for advice on what to eat, and she recommends a dish filled with peanuts, soy, and dairy. If the waitress never first considered the customer's needs, she may be surprised when she finds out he is allergic to everything in that dish. This advice may have resulted in the customer getting sick and hospitalized. If the waitress took the time to understand the customer's needs and managed the entire process from the menu to the table, she could have ensured a happier and healthier customer. A holistic approach may have resulted in advising the customer to try a meal he is not allergic to. She also would have ensured the chef didn't accidentally put any of those ingredients into the dish. Thus, if the waitress really wanted to help the customer, she would have done more than give just advice. She would have learned about the customer and his needs and managed the whole process from start to finish.

In a simple view, financial advisors or consultants can be separate from financial managers as their only job is to give financial advice. However, this viewpoint is inconsistent with the goal of finance as presented in this book, because the act of giving advice alone generally will not maximize wealth. A true financial advisor, a practitioner of finance, is an individual who gives advice based on the purpose and goals of the science in which he operates.

On the other hand, a financial planner is an individual who plans to continuously maximize the wealth of an individual, a group, or an organization. From a comprehensive viewpoint, a financial planner must be a part of every financial activity that will affect the bottom line for an individual, a group, or an organization. If one looks at a simplistic viewpoint of a financial planner's role, then his job can be, arguably, only to produce a financial plan. However, experience in this field dictates that a financial planner who is not involved with the entire wealth-management process can hardly ever produce a plan that will continuously maximize wealth. In practice, financial planners are generally the glue that holds the entire wealth-management team together. This team may include various types of attorneys, accountants, and insurance specialists. The comprehensive financial planner manages this whole process from start to finish.

From a comprehensive perspective, financial managers, financial consultants, financial advisors, and financial planners are the same thing. All of these people should be involved in the whole management process in order to maximize the wealth of the clients they represent. Focusing on only one part of the management process while neglecting the difference can be detrimental to the client's bottom line.

## Failure to Plan Is a Sure Plan to Fail

Now that the various terms financial managers are called have been clarified we are in a better position to understand financial planning. **Financial planning is the act of planning to maximize wealth for an individual, a group, or an organization. Contrarily, economic planning is the act of planning to maximize wealth for a nation or a division of a nation.**

There is an old wise saying that failure to plan is a sure plan to fail. Without plans in place, for both the short and the long term, financial and economic goals may be met only by coincidence. For example consider the process one must go through to become a successful brain surgeon by the time she is thirty-five years of age. Every step of her life must be planned, from grade school to the graduate levels of college and beyond. If she makes one wrong turn with her plan, then each negative action may cost her more time until the goal is fulfilled. A few wrong turns and she may never achieve her goals. *However, to reach one's goals without a plan would require an extraordinary, unlikely sequence of random events.*

Assuming that one starts with no wealth, he must go through a significant amount of obstacles to reach his financial goals. He must plan every major step of his life to become wealthy. Even with a plan, achieving financial goals may be difficult, as life always throws new roadblocks in the way. Thus, a financial plan is in a state of constant shifting. Every major event in life can be a cause to create a whole new plan. That is why a financial planner must be prepared to be flexible.

As noted above, holistic financial planners do more than just financial planning. They must manage the whole process, from the analysis of a client's goals, objectives, and risk to implementation and the follow up phase. They also must be prepared to revise the entire plan if needed. Paid financial planners are agents of their clients. However, an individual can be his own financial planner if he educates himself on the science of finance. Nevertheless, even if you need assistance with maximizing your wealth you should still be involved in the financial planning and management process on some level. After all, who should care more about your money than you?

Financial planning must consider the chronological goals of the entity. For example, a person may plan on paying off credit card debt in six months, buying a house and raising a family in five years, and retiring in thirty years. There are three different time-frames the individual needs to plan for in this case: short-term, intermediate-term, and long-term. Of course this is a simple example; there are many different degrees of time for which one can plan. A customized plan segmented in time frames is appropriate for all individuals, groups, and organizations in order to meet their financial goals.

Financial planning is an important part of maximizing wealth. Even though it is necessary, it is still only a part of the entire management process. Thus, in practice, the role of holistic financial planners is more comprehensive than the title. Planners are actually acting as financial managers who oversee the whole wealth-management process.

# CHAPTER 21

# Financial Statements

Financial statements are one of the major tools to help individuals, groups, and organizations meet their financial goals. They are a place for all financial data to be assembled and organized. This data is crucial because it provides a foundation for the major decisions financial managers need to make. Specifically, financial statements help to provide an assessment of the entity's financial health. Any student of finance needs to learn four major financial statements: the balance sheet, the income statement, the cash flow statement, and the statement of stockholder equity. The major variables used for each are generally consistent for all entities.

All the financial statements are derived from similar data. Collectively they can be viewed as four different perspectives of similar information. Consider a still image of a basket of fruit in the middle of a rectangular table. The basket has a variety of different fruit including oranges, apples, bananas, and pears. If you were to stop at each corner of the table and look at it, you would see the same basket of fruit. However, each corner will offer a different perspective and allow you to see the same image in a different way.

For example, suppose you stand at the northwest corner of the table. From this viewpoint you may see only oranges. If you do not go around the table, you will not know there are also apples, bananas, and pears in the basket. Suppose instead you stand at the southeast corner of the table. From this viewpoint you will see only bananas. If you do not go around the table, you will not know there are also oranges, apples, and pears in the basket. This scenario is analogous to analyzing financial statements. The financial data is the basket of fruit, and the financial statements are the different viewpoints from the corners of the table. We can assess the financial health of a company with one statement. However, the information may not be complete until all perspectives are considered.

Let's take a closer look at the four major financial statements. The balance sheet considers assets, liabilities, and net worth (this term varies depending on who is being considered). This is debatably the most important statement out of all four, as the net worth, the bottom line of the statement, is one way of describing wealth (as used in this book). The income statement considers net income, which is a result of income minus expenses. The cash flow statement views the financial data from the perspective of how cash moves in and out of an entity. This is represented through cash inflows and outflows.

Finally, there's the statement of stockholder equity, which provides detailed information on the equity portion of the balance sheet. Please note that all of the statements are linked together in some way. For example, the cash transactions found in the statement of cash flows are also in the cash balance section of the balance sheet.

There are many different ways to use the financial statements to assess financial health. When the focus is on a company, *fundamental analysis* is the term for analyzing the financial data, specifically from the four major statements above. There are many advocates of fundamental analysis including many of the best equity investors of the twentieth century.

One way to apply fundamental analysis is to use financial ratios, of which there are many.

Each ratio serves a purpose, generally, to measure risk, return, or both. For example, the current ratio measures short-term risk; the formula is current assets (*current* means short-term) divided by current liabilities. If the current ratio has a result of one or above, that means the company has enough money to pay its bills, which is a good sign.

Earnings per share (EPS) is another important financial ratio. It measures return. The formula is net income minus preferred dividends divided by the weighted average of shares outstanding. The result is an important and widely used number that shows how much profit was earned on each share. This number is also a component of the PE or the price to earnings ratio, which measures risk and return. The formula is market price per common share divided by earnings per share. A higher PE ratio generally means an investment is riskier but can possibly earn more return. There are other ways to interpret PE. Some view it as how long it will take for an investor to earn back his money.

A discussion of financial statements would not be complete without pro forma statements. These are forecasts of financial statements. The statements we looked at above assume historical financial data is used. However, it is equally important to comprise a forecast of all of these statements to get a good idea of what one's financial health will be like in the future. Of course this doesn't come with a guarantee, but if there is minimal forecasting error, it can be very helpful.

Most people are already aware of forecasted financial statements with thanks to the buzz word *budget*. When someone tells you to put together a budget, she is referring to a forecasted income statement. On this statement you make a forecast of what your income and expenses will be in the future. This will be helpful for you when planning your future financial needs and maximizing your wealth.

*Fundamental analysis* is the analysis of financial statements generally for a company. *Technical analysis* is another school of thought that considers financial statements and financial ratios as irrelevant. To a technical analyst, only patterns in historical price and volume movements are important. Other analysts agree that a combination of the two types is most effective. A student of finance should understand that these analyses are just tools to help meet the goals of finance. **There are no guarantees that any form of analysis or technique for selecting investments will result in a profit.**

# CHAPTER 22

# Financial Theories Overview

Many theories and models have been created since Harry Markowitz explained portfolio selection. The following is a simple overview of several major theories that are a foundation of finance as currently taught in universities. This overview is not extensive: it is only to give you a sample of the types of theories you may encounter if you take a finance class. These theories can be found in various subsciences of finance depending on what the subject matter is. For example, CAPM is found in almost any type of personal or corporate finance class. The theories of Modigliani and Miller, however, are generally only found in corporate finance.

Take an objective approach when viewing these theories. There are many practitioners, including some of the greatest modern investors, who disagree with many of them. The best approach is to learn both sides of the argument before forming your own conclusions.

Harry Markowitz first produced an article on portfolio selection in 1952. This event propelled modern academic finance. His model explained very common terms in an academic format. Basically he demonstrated the relationship between risk and return graphically, proving that diversification is an effective strategy. By combining assets that demonstrate the highest levels of expected return for given levels of risk, one can create an optimal portfolio that is called the efficient frontier.

William Sharpe, a student of Markowitz, took Markowitz's theory to the next level about a decade later. He had many contributions to finance but he is mainly known for the capital asset pricing model (CAPM): expected return of an asset equals the risk-free rate plus beta times the expected return of the market minus the risk-free rate. This may at first seem scary, but it is conquerable with a little practice. I have written this formula out because it is one of the most commonly used formulas in almost every financial text. Sharpe's CAPM explains beta, a tool that measures the market return, and derives the expected return of an investment while considering the risk and return of the market. Also note that about a decade later, an alternative to CAPM was created, called arbitrage pricing theory by Stephen Ross.

A financial student may also encounter the Modigliani and Miller propositions, which focus mainly on corporate finance. They center on determining the best capital structure of a firm: this is the balance between debt, equity, and retained earnings. Their propositions mainly argue that it does not matter where the funds come from as long as the end goal of maximizing wealth is met.

Another major theory is the efficient market hypothesis (EMH) created by Eugene Fama around 1970. Fama proposed a groundbreaking way of viewing the marketplace that is still strongly debated by financial academics and practitioners alike. The essence of his work is that the market is efficient and all stock price movements are random (this is called the random walk). EMH translates to stating that investors cannot outperform the average of the stock market in the long run. It's an interesting theory and has some significant data to demonstrate its effectiveness. However, there are many successful investors, including Benjamin Graham, Peter Lynch, and Warren Buffett, whose successful track records provide evidence that the market may be efficient most of the time but not all of the time. As with all other theories in academia, it is good to listen to both sides of the argument before making your own conclusions.

# CHAPTER 23

# Finance and Math

Many potential students never take finance because they are afraid of the math involved. Admittedly, there may be some very difficult math problems in finance. However, with proper practice, these problems can become second nature.

The purpose of this chapter is to give you a better idea of the relationship between math and finance. **The basics of finance should not include anything more than arithmetic and the fundamentals of algebra.** The type of math used in finance is sometimes called *business math. At the fundamental level, if one knows how to count their money then they are on the right track.*

The common numerical language of finance is percentages. If you can speak it, you will be able to calculate important variables such as rate of return. Percentages allow you to calculate and compare investments easily, amongst other things. This activity is much more difficult with any dollar amount. For example, it means very little to make a comparison between a potential profit of $1,000 and $10,000 if you don't know what the profit is in terms of a percent of your initial investment. You may only need to invest $100 to earn $1,000 profit (1,000 percent return) or $10,000 to earn $10,000 profit (100 percent return). It may appear that the higher dollar amount is better until the percent tells the true story: 1,000 percent is clearly better than 100 percent no matter what the dollar amount is.

An investor may choose the wrong investment, based on return only, if he does not calculate the return in terms of percentages, which is really easy. In the above example, $1,000 divided by $100 = 10, meaning you will make ten times more than your original investment. To convert this number to a percent you just move the decimal two places to the right and you have 1,000 percent.

Once you have mastered percentages, you need to master a very important calculation called *total rate of return*. This is the total return of all wealth gained for a specific activity, which could be gambling, investing, or hard labor. Generally, this term refers to total rate of return on an investment (sometimes called *ROI*). In the above example, the total rates of return were 1,000 percent and 100 percent. These problems are very simple in form, but they can become increasingly complex when more details are added to a scenario, for example dividends, rental income, and taxes.

There are also plenty of statistics used in finance. Statistics plays a major role in quantifying risk for various investments.

These problems can get a little tricky, especially if you have to measure risk for large portfolios of investments.

Math is also used in finance to calculate financial ratios, which are actually very easy to figure out if you have all of the formulas. The current ratio is as simple as taking the current assets and dividing them by the current liabilities, for example $6,000,000 divided by $3,000,000 = 2. These numbers are generally given on financial statements. In this case, two means an entity has twice as much short-term assets as short-term debts. In other words, it has more than enough money to pay the bills this month.

Financial math can get a little tricky when calculating the time value of money. The *time value of money* is a really important part of financial problems, and advanced students must master it. There will be a separate chapter coming up to explain the basics of these problems.

A student of finance should invest in a financial calculator or a computer program for a better learning experience. Financial calculators are great for performing calculations quickly and cross-checking solutions performed manually. I encourage students to try all calculations manually first in order to understand how the solutions are derived. Too many financial students become dependent on easy answers derived with computer assistance. However, by practicing the problems manually, a student may understand and appreciate the mechanics of the problem better.

A financial student should also want to learn basic accounting, as the math involved there is the same as in finance. We have already classified accounting in the newly proposed categories of finance. Thus, any math that is part of accounting must also be a part of finance.

At the advanced levels of finance, one can enjoy the beauty of more-difficult math problems, as in financial calculus. This may be required knowledge for a specific academic finance program. However, for everyday practical purposes, a potential student should not be intimidated. This type of high level math is not commonly used. If you can focus on mastering the basics of financial math as noted above, that should be sufficient at the fundamental levels.

# CHAPTER 24

# Investing Overview

## Tough Terminology

In order to understand the dynamics of finance, there must be an examination of the subject of investing. There are many definitions of investing and related concepts throughout academia, some of which conflict. I am not content with these definitions, and the following analysis reflects my attempt to provide a better way to view these concepts.

The irony of my analysis is that we're discussing some of the basic concepts in finance, yet the tiniest details can completely alter the meaning of the terms we use. This analysis should help you to examine the fundamentals of one of the most important aspects of finance.

What is investing? There are many ways to define it, but for our purposes it's **the act of currently owning an investment**. However, this statement is incomplete, as it doesn't define what an investment is. The most intelligent minds in economics and finance throughout history have wrestled with this term. However, I think the following definition may be as comprehensive as possible:

**An investment is any asset currently owned, tangible or intangible, that is not associated with playing any perceived ongoing game of chance and is intended to maximize wealth based on acceptable levels of time and risk.** Stated in full, **investing is the act of currently owning any asset, tangible or intangible, that is not associated with playing any perceived ongoing game of chance and is intended to maximize wealth based on acceptable levels of time and risk.**

There are certainly many details that need to be analyzed in this intricate term. Let's begin!

To review, an asset is anything owned and a liability is anything owed. An investment is an asset, hence one must own it. For example, if you invest in real estate then you must own the real estate investment. It is not your investment if someone else owns it. In that case, it is the other person's investment.

Also, an investment is not a liability. All debts are considered something that you owe. By definition, the act of owing something is not going to maximize wealth. However, the funds, considered assets, that are derived from the debt can purchase investments that can maximize wealth.

Investment assets must be currently owned. If a person owned an investment in the past and sold it then it is not his investment any more. However, it can be accurately stated that it *was* his investment before. The same rule applies to the future. An asset that has not been purchased yet is not an investment. It may be considered a potential investment assuming all other criteria of an investment are met.

An investment is allowed to be tangible or intangible for maximum flexibility of the term. A tangible investment is easier to understand because one can use their senses to perceive the object, particularly the sense of touch. For example, real estate is made of bricks and mortar we can see and touch. We hear the floor-boards squeak when we walk on them. We can also taste the water from the building's faucets and smell the aromas of the house.

There are other tangible assets that can be considered potential investments. These include paintings, coin collections, antiques, automobiles, and furniture. Actually, any tangible object can be considered an investment as long as it meets the remaining criteria for an investment. The list is so long we could dedicate a whole book to exploring the subject and still come up short.

A lottery ticket is a tricky example of a tangible asset that may clarify the term investment. Although some may consider it a tangible asset, it is not an investment if it is bought for the purpose of participating in an ongoing game of chance (this term will be explained soon). However, if one held an antique lottery ticket for the purpose of maximizing wealth as a collectible, this may be considered an investment because the lottery ticket is no longer associated with any ongoing game of chance. In other words, because the game of chance is over, the ticket may now be considered an investment if the owner's intention is to maximize her wealth. The antique ticket may have considerable appreciation as an asset because it is now an antique collectible.

Many different types of intangible assets may qualify as investments. This also depends on how you define an asset. For example, some may view education as an asset. Going to school and improving your skills through learning may result in making you a significant amount of money in the future. In such a case, education is a successful investment as the asset proves to maximize wealth. Other intangible investments include copyrights, patents, trademarks, and goodwill.

An investment must not be associated with playing any perceived ongoing game of chance because it would be considered gambling. **Gambling is the act of playing a perceived ongoing game of chance.** *Games of chance* are created for pure amusement purposes. Amusement is the primary goal of playing a game of chance, whereas maximizing wealth is an inferior goal. For a gambler, the thrill is more important than the money. Investors, on the other hand, always have maximizing wealth as a primary goal, inferior to none.

Thus, gambling is not investing although sometimes it may appear that way. Some games of chance include lotteries, poker, roulette, slot machines, etc. Some may argue that the stock market is a game of chance, but it's an investment in a business. If you buy stock, you are essentially buying a proportionate amount of ownership in a company. However, if one purchases shares of stock from the perspective that it is a game of chance, it is not an investment. In this case the owner's perception of the stock market disqualifies the asset from being considered an investment. Unfortunately, this is such a common situation, as countless so-called investors do not invest in a stock market but rather bet as if it were a Las Vegas casino.

An investment must be intended to maximize wealth based on acceptable levels of time and risk. It can't just have a probability of maximizing wealth; it must include the owner's determination for this asset to perform with great financial consequences. As an investment is a subject of analysis in the science of finance, it must also be viewed consistently with the big picture in mind. If the owner's purpose is to minimize wealth, it would be contrary to the major goal of finance and thus inconsistent with the goal of investing.

An investment should also maximize wealth based on acceptable levels of time. Every investor may invest specific funds for a specific time-frame they can acceptably commit to. For example, an investor can reasonably commit to investing 10 percent of his assets for twenty years or more. This block of money can be allocated to investments that are not very liquid and are theoretically riskier for example, real estate. The investor who invests in riskier assets hopes to earn an additional premium for taking on additional risk.

On the other hand, this same investor may also be able to reasonably commit to investing 50 percent of his assets for only one year or less. This money could go into short-term, illiquid, theoretically safer investments such as savings accounts or money markets. Each investor may have separate acceptable time commitments for the various parts of his assets that can be invested. Thus, he should intend to maximize his wealth with every investment while considering the time-frame committed to it.

Finally, the investment should maximize wealth based on acceptable levels of risk. For example, an individual who is risk tolerant, meaning she can tolerate higher levels of risk, may be able to pursue traditionally risky investments, for example stocks. However, an individual who is risk adverse, meaning that he can tolerate only lower levels of risk, may be more suitable to investing in traditionally safe investments such as money markets or bonds. Each should intend to maximize his or her wealth based on investments that are suitable for his or her level of risk tolerance.

Many other definitions of an investment are missing key elements. For example, we may define an investment as a sacrifice of current dollars for future dollars. This is incomplete, at minimum, because it leaves a window for gamblers to be included. A gambler at a casino is essentially sacrificing current dollars with the intention of making future dollars. *There must be a way to exclude gambling from a definition of investing to capture the true intended effect of the term.* This was a crucial part of the considerations when developing the above definition.

One may define an investment as the current commitment of money or other resources in the expectation of reaping future benefits. This is incomplete because it also leaves a window for gamblers to be included. A gambler playing roulette is committing money, via betting, with the expectation of reaping future benefits. This definition also does not capture the true intended effect of the term.

Another unsatisfying definition commonly considers an investment to be funds set aside for long-term needs. Investments can also be for short-term and intermediate-term needs, as noted above in the analysis of time commitment. With a short-term investment, such as a money market mutual fund, it is designed for short term needs; an investor generally may not commit to it for more than one year. Stating that investments are only for long-term needs would exclude a wide range of investments including money markets, CDs, and interest-bearing checking accounts.

There are some strange scenarios that create loopholes in the definition of investing as used in this book. However, for the majority of cases it should be sufficient. One of the major improvements from this new definition is the clarification of gambling and its elimination from the term. To understand this improvement better, let's compare the major differences between three commonly confused types of people associated with investing: the investor, the speculator, and the gambler.

The characteristics of an investor should be apparent at this point. **An investor is an individual, a group, an organization, or a nation that currently owns an asset, tangible or intangible, that is not associated with playing any perceived ongoing game of chance and is intended to maximize wealth based on acceptable levels of time and risk.** Any entity can be considered an investor. However, when considering national investments the focus of the science shifts from finance to economics as it is more consistent with our definition of economics found in the "What Is Economics?" chapter presented earlier in this book.

Speculators are often defined inconsistently in modern literature and practice. However, here the main difference is that **a speculator is an investor who takes a very large amount of risk with the intention of receiving a very large return.** A limitation of this is that there are subjective degrees of risk one needs to take to be considered a speculator. Nevertheless, including speculators as a subcategory of investors helps to create a more consistent application of these terms in finance.

**A gambler is any individual, group, organization, or nation that plays a perceived ongoing game of chance.** The word *perceived* is very important in this definition because the gamblers have to believe what they are funding is an ongoing game of chance. For example, if a person invests in the stock market unintelligently but believes he is not playing a game of chance, he may be considered an investor. He may be a bad investor for making poor decisions, but this is not the same as a gambler. This person knows the difference between a game of chance and real markets.

Although various marketplaces may appear to be games of chance at times, make no mistake, they are not the same. A market is a place for conducting business. Business is not a game. Games are for people to play and business is for people to work. *A gambler bets and an investor invests, and the two are as different as night and day.* This is the major reason why I have created such a comprehensive definition: in order to separate the two concepts. Without the separation, the subject of investing may always contain the probability of a negative association with gambling. This effect can have significant secondary consequences by reducing the credibility of the science of finance, from which it springs.

# Saving and Investing

There is a difference between saving and investing, and it is often been confused. Economists have debated it for centuries with mixed results. My interpretation, for the sake of clarity, is that investing is a part of savings, not the other way around. To understand this better, we must first explore the difference between spending and consumption.

Wealth has been defined in this book as net worth, but there is another way to look at it via a method used by many economists. Wealth can be defined by the elementary quality from which it is derived, namely labor. Wealth can be viewed as the result of the accumulation of sacrificed, gifted, inherited, and won labor and its total rate of return, including interest and appreciation for an individual, a group, an organization, or a nation. Of course, this would also be net of any debt owed. Thus, wealthy people have made their fortunes from their own hard work, the hard work of others, their winnings from activities such as gambling or lawsuits, and/ or the total rate of return from some or all of these components. With that stated, when these entities decide to spend their fortunes, they also choose to consume goods and services now versus later. It is their choice whether to spend their wealth on goods and services frugally or to be careless and consume all of their fortune at once.

When an individual, a group, an organization, or a nation decides not to spend its wealth now, and thus consume goods or services later, it chooses to save. **Simply put, saving is the act of accumulating wealth for the purposes of consuming goods and services in the future.** For example, if you were to save

$100 then you would be choosing to use this money to buy goods or services at some time in the future. The range of time can be as little as seconds (as ridiculous as it sounds) to many years.

A major difference between saving and investing is based on the difference between the terms *accumulating* and *maximizing*. Saving focuses only on accumulating wealth while investing focuses on maximizing parts or all of the accumulated wealth. **Thus, investing is always a part of saving, but saving may be more inclusive than just investing.** *A part or all of everything you save can be invested, but everything you invest is not always all of your savings.*

The following formula reflects this statement: savings minus investment = savings that is not invested. For example, if you save $1,000 then you may decide to invest $800 of it and retain the other $200 in cash. The $800 investment is derived from the total amount saved of $1,000. However, the $200 remaining in the form of hoarded cash is savings that is not considered to be invested yet. The above analysis does not include capital. Please review the chapter "Capital Overview" to see how capital fits into this formula.

Some or all parts of the accumulated savings may never earn a rate of return. This includes capital appreciation as well as earnings from an interest rate. Thus, savings that are not invested can only grow as a result of accumulating more sacrificed, gifted, inherited, and won labor and its already-earned total rate of return. This definition allows assets to be included in savings that were once investments but are no longer currently owned for purposes of investing. Say an individual invested $10,000 and sold it when it was worth $20,000, but decided not to invest the $20,000. In this case this money would still be considered savings, but it would not be considered an investment anymore.

What can be considered saving but not investing? Generally the answer is hoarded cash, or cash that is saved and not placed in any investment. How it is stored is not important — it can be anywhere from in your pocket-book to under the bed (just don't hoard cash in a usable oven, as it is likely to get cooked accidentally). This cash is not going to make you any money by just sitting there, wherever there is. Although hoarded cash is still an asset, as it is a store of wealth, it is not designed by itself to maximize wealth (ignoring the possibility of currency fluctuations). This is the job of investing, which awakens the sleeping hoarded cash and puts it to work. If you can imagine money as people, investing would be the result of the accumulated, sacrificed labor of your money.

# CHAPTER 25

# Risk and Return

Understanding the concepts of risk and return is necessary for any successful current or potential financier or financialist. Risk and return have a unique relationship with each other, commonly called the *risk-return tradeoff*. This is best demonstrated by a moving car. Suppose you start driving on a highway to get to your destination. If you drive at the speed limit then you will be there in an hour. If you double the speed limit then you will be there in a half hour. The faster you go, the quicker you will get to your destination.

However, the faster you go the worse the outcome can be if you get in an accident. If you crash at sixty miles per hour, you have a better chance of walking away with little injury. If you crash at two hundred miles per hour, your odds of survival are significantly reduced. You have to weigh your risk against the potential return. Is it worth getting to your destination in half the time if your risk of death may double?

This is a tradeoff everyone must face in life for a variety of issues, including financial situations. Assume all investors have target destinations of maximized wealth. Just like the driver, they will have to make decisions about how much faster they are willing to drive their financial cars. How much risk are they willing to take to get to their destination? If they take more risks, they may get there faster. However, if their investments crash, they may lose all of their wealth. Alternatively, if they decide not to take much risk and invest conservatively, just like the driver who stays at the speed limit or under, they may get to their destinations more slowly, and if their investments crash then the results may not be as devastating.

**The general lesson of the risk-return tradeoff can be summed up as: the more risk you take, the more return you can make or lose.** Financial managers must make decisions that incorporate the risk-return tradeoff so they are consistently meeting their financial goals. The key word is *consistently*. If a financial manager slips up one time, even though he may have an excellent track record, that mistake could result in bankruptcy.

Why must investors always consider risk and return for every potential investment? Let's suppose there are two investments, A and B. In the first scenario, only return will be analyzed. Risk will be assumed to be nonexistent. Investment A produces an annual return of 100 percent, and investment B produces an annual return of 5 percent. Based on the data given, and assuming that no other data is relevant, investors wouldn't hesitate to choose investment A. It will double its money in a year while investment B makes a mere 5 percent. If you have invested $1,000, you will make a profit of $1,000 with investment A and only $50 with investment B. Ignoring risk, investment A is a better choice because it has a higher rate of return.

Now let's add risk in to the scenario. Suppose investment A has a 10 percent probability of producing an annual return of 100 percent, and a 90 percent probability of losing the principle (the money originally invested). Investment B has a 100 percent probability of producing an annual return of 5 percent and a 0 percent probability of loss of principle. These little facts can change an investor's entire outlook on these investments. Investment A doesn't look that great anymore. Based on the data given, and assuming that no other data is relevant, most investors wouldn't hesitate to choose investment B because investment A is too risky. Investment B, although it only pays a mere 5 percent a year, is much safer.

There may be a situation where investment A can be desirable. In that case, investing a small percentage in investment A may be a good way to diversify all of your assets. However, it generally would not be wise to invest all or a large part of your wealth into investment A and risk losing everything just to get to your destination a little sooner.

Every successful investor should always consider both risk and return when selecting an investment. This is a fundamental lesson in finance, though it is often ignored. Too many bad investors look only at the returns of an investment without considering how much risk must be taken in order to earn them. These investors always get too focused on what they can make instead of what they can lose. A good way of thinking is: if you can't afford to lose your money, don't invest it in risky investments.

Risk has many definitions. In academia it is considered the variability of returns associated with a given asset. In other words, if a stock is priced at $20 a share and then it increases to $200 a share ten months later, it is probably considered risky because it has a wide range of possible prices in a short amount of time ($200 - $20 = $180 range). Many successful investors have a problem with this definition because they view volatility as a good thing. If an investment has a high variability of return, many investors feel they can use various types of analysis, e.g. technical analysis, to predict the future price of the stock more accurately.

**Risk will be defined here as the chance of loss.** There are so many different types of risk in this world: spiritual, ethical, physical, financial, and so on. Types of financial risks include inflation risk, market risk, interest rate risk, tax risk, business risk, and exchange rate risk. A risk-tolerant person can endure a significant level of a specific type of risk. Contrarily, a risk-adverse person cannot endure a significant level of a specific type of risk.

Some people may be highly tolerant in one category and highly adverse in another. For example, many people engage in a significant amount of physical risk, such as sky-diving or sleeping on the side of a mountain for fun. They are considered risk tolerant of physical risk. Yet when it comes to their money, they may be extremely afraid to take any risks. They are considered risk adverse of financial risk.

*Total return* is easier to define, as it is quantifiable (usually in percentage form). **Total return is the total gain or loss made on**

**an investment over a specified period of time.** This includes all appreciation, dividends, and other forms of cash inflows and outflows. The total return is expressed best as a percentage because that makes it easier to compare to other investments. Total return can be calculated using historical data. One can also make a forecast of the return that is most expected in the future. However, this process involves some complex concepts and formulas that are beyond the scope of this book.

The natural qualities of risk and return can be altered when the concept of time is introduced. For example, an investment that appears risky in the short run may seem less so when viewed from in the long run. A true long-term investment (defined here as ten years or more) such as a stock can be very risky if bought for short-term purposes. An investor may lose a lot of money when buying and selling stocks before the companies have developed into more profitable investments.

**Investments are like fruit; they need to ripen before you can enjoy their benefits.** If you sell an investment too quickly, it may not provide the desirable amount of return. On the other hand, if you exercise patience on the right investment while it is ripening then it is not as risky. The impatient investor must settle for whatever gain or loss he can earn in a short duration. The patient investor can calmly sit through all kinds of price adjustments until it is the right time to sell.

Finally, a quick discussion on diversification is in order. **Diversification is strategically combining different investments for the purpose of reducing the overall risk of a portfolio (which is a collection of investments).** One of the most acceptable ways to diversify is to combine investments that move in opposite directions, or what we call *negatively correlated*. Let's suppose several individuals open a café that sells only hot beverages. Assuming the business is successfully managed, let's suppose it produces a 100 percent return on profit during the six cold weather months. During the first year of business, the owners quickly learn a hard lesson: less people buy hot beverages in the summertime. Let's exaggerate and say they made a 0 percent return on profit during all six hot weather months.

Diversification can help these owners. If they introduce cold versions of their beverages in the hot weather months — maybe iced coffee and iced tea — then they may be able to produce a 100 percent profit all year round. Specifically, the new cold beverage could produce a 100 percent return in hot weather months and a 0 percent return in cold weather months. This is good news, because if the company sells both products it reduces the risk of earning nothing throughout the course of the year.

This example of diversification demonstrates how a portfolio of investments can reduce the investor's risk. *Few successful financialists or financiers will doubt the significance of diversification. However, the number of investments one needs to reach optimal diversification is debatable.* Proponents of the efficient market hypothesis tend to argue for a number that may equate to the whole market, like a market index fund. This may consist of 100 to more than 5,000 investments. However, many successful investors agree that a small investor may need as little as three to five investments to be diversified. These investors believe they can spend more energy on fewer investments, and that this concentration of labor makes one a specialist. That may result in less risk.

# CHAPTER 26

# Financial Investments Overview

There are many different types of investments to choose from. As we've already discussed, an investment is any asset currently owned, tangible or intangible, that is not associated with playing any perceived ongoing game of chance and is intended to maximize wealth based on acceptable levels of time and risk. The major types of investments include, but are not limited to: money markets, Treasury bills, interest bearing checking or savings accounts, certificate of deposits (CDs), bonds, stocks, mutual funds, collectibles, real estate, options, forwards, futures, swaps, and warrants. We'll get back to the definitions of these terms in a minute.

There are many ways to classify investments in order to understand them better. First, we can separate them in terms of the recommended time-frame. Money markets, Treasury bills, interest-bearing checking or savings accounts, CDs, and money market mutual funds are all designed for the short term, or approximately less than one year. There are also some investments designed for the intermediate term, or approximately two to five years. These include CDs, certain mutual funds (for example balanced funds), and Treasury notes. Bonds, stocks, certain mutual funds, collectibles, real estate, options, forwards, futures, swaps, and warrants are designed for the long term, or approximately more than ten years.

Please note investors may have unique skill sets that allow them to make more returns in shorter-than-recommended time frames. For example, a person who specializes in real estate may invest in a property with the intention of capturing the appreciation and flipping it in five years or less. A person without this experience and knowledge who does not specialize in real estate may need to wait ten years or more to accomplish the same task. The specialist is trained to know how long investments may take to ripen, and may be better prepared to maximize their return at the exact moment of opportunity.

Investments can also be classified in terms of liquidity, which is how fast an asset can convert to cash. Some investments are considered highly liquid, which means they can be converted to cash very quickly. Cash is the quintessential liquid asset and the whole reason the term was created. The benefit of transforming any asset into cash form is that it gives the asset a value in real time. You don't need to worry about losing value from an emergency sale for cash, unlike with some other assets (ignoring currency fluctuations). Some liquid investments include: money markets, money market mutual funds, interest bearing checking or savings accounts, CDs, and Treasury bills. Some of these are more liquid than others. For example an interest-bearing checking account may convert to cash easier than a CD, which may charge a penalty for cashing out early.

Some investments are considered highly illiquid, which means they cannot be converted to cash very quickly. Illiquid assets generally include bonds, stocks, mutual funds, collectibles, real estate, options, forwards, futures, swaps, and warrants. There is a high correlation between the risk associated with each of these investments and liquidity. You may have noticed that most of the illiquid investments I mentioned are also long-term investments. Investors generally buy long-term investments because they are prepared to wait many years to capture the maximum returns. Investors are paid risk premiums for waiting and for the lack of ability to convert their investments to cash quickly. For example, if one needs to sell commercial real estate now instead of the expected wait time of ten years then he may have to settle for as little as 30 to 50 percent of the current market value. Other smart investors will know that this investor is in an uncomfortable financial position. They may attempt to take advantage of this opportunity by offering a price much less than the expected future value.

Some investments can be either liquid or illiquid depending on their form. For example, inventory is an investment to a business owner and may be liquid or illiquid depending on what the business is. If the owner sells baked goods then the inventory turnover time is very small — generally less than one day. This translates to the inventory being highly liquid, thus easily convertible to cash. Contrarily, if the owner sells redeveloped investment properties or luxury yachts then it may take a long time to sell the inventory and convert it to cash. In this case the inventory is considered illiquid.

**It is crucial to understand that most investment types have useful purposes under certain appropriate circumstances.** For example, aggressive stocks may be appropriate investments for a risk-tolerant twenty-year-old looking to invest for the long term. However, they are generally not good for a risk-adverse seventy-year-old retiree looking for income. If an investment is created and not useful, eventually it will cease to have demand and disappear from the investment world.

Such investments have specific tradeoffs. *There is no one perfect investment for everyone.* Every individual, group, organization, and nation will have different investment needs that may only be met by a specific type of investment. *Some sacrifices must always be made in order to obtain some benefit.* For example, with an interest-bearing checking account the investor cannot write as many checks as he would be able to on a noninterest-bearing checking account. The investor who wants to earn the interest must sacrifice the ability to write checks as frequently as an individual who is not paid interest on his checking account.

Money market and savings accounts are very similar. They both pay small amounts of interest compared to other investments and are short term in nature, and the principle is generally guaranteed. CDs are also short-term investments that pay interest. They are issued in a variety of terms but may charge a penalty if the investment is withdrawn before maturity.

Bonds are investments where funds are loaned to an entity for a period in return for interest. Bonds are considered debt and must be paid back by the issuer. There are all different types of bond issuers including corporations and various types of governments. Credit is used to assess bond issuers to determine how much risk investors will take if they invest in the bonds. High-quality bonds are lower risk but generally pay lower interest rates, and lower-quality or junk bonds are higher risk but pay higher interest rates.

There are two major categories of stock: preferred and common stockholders. If a company goes bankrupt, the common stockholder is the last person to get paid. The common stockholders take the most risk because what they are buying is ownership of the company. Like any business owners, they take most of the risks but they can earn most of the rewards (see the risk-return tradeoff found in the "Risk and Return" chapter). Preferred stockholders don't have as much risk as common stockholders because they get paid dividends first, and in the case of bankruptcy they are a higher priority when it comes to getting paid from the proceeds of the company's liquidation.

Collectibles can be almost any type of asset as long as it is consistent with the above definition of an investment. This can include sports cards, antique cars, and various memorabilia. The list of potential collectibles is almost endless, but a collectible can only be profitable if an investor can find a buyer who will pay the required premium for holding on to the asset.

Real estate can include commercial as well as residential property. Commercial property has businesses as occupants. Residential property has individuals and families as occupants.

There are many ways to invest in real estate, including buying to rent and buying to flip (redevelop and sell). Generally real estate is an illiquid, long-term asset that requires a considerable amount of time devoted to its management.

Derivatives are very complex investments that generally include options, forwards, futures, swaps, and warrants. In general, these investments are risky, designed for the long term, and illiquid. Any further analysis of these investments is beyond the scope of this book.

A mutual fund is a portfolio of many of the different types of investments noted above. A portfolio is a collection of various investments. Any investor can design her own portfolio, but it may take a significantly higher threshold of wealth to produce the effect of a mutual fund with a lower initial investment minimum. For example, a mutual fund may have 100 stocks and 100 bonds inside, and it may cost only $3,000 to invest in it. To accomplish the same effect, one may need a portfolio of $100,000 in assets, though the amount can vary. Mutual funds are an illustration of diversification, as risk may be significantly reduced from combining many assets together.

Retirement plans are a commonly confused issue concerning investments. Like 401(k)s and IRAs, they are not investments. They are tax-deferred placeholders called *investment vehicles* for the investments. Investments are the assets that build the wealth and are placed inside of these retirement plans. Thus you can have a stock mutual fund inside a 401(k) retirement plan. In this case the 401(k) is the retirement plan that ensures the investment inside, the stock mutual fund, is tax-deferred.

Various types of investments can be classified, at minimum, in terms of risk, time-frame, and liquidity. Each investment may be suitable for different people in different circumstances. As wealth builds, an entity may want to consider diversifying their portfolio to reduce risk exposure.

# CHAPTER 27

# The Marketplace and Finance

In modern finance, most of the literature refers only to the securities market when discussing "markets" or the "financial markets." However, this is not a satisfying description of the financial marketplace as it ignores many assets that are not considered securities. Securities include stocks, bonds, and derivatives but generally do not include certain investments like real estate or collectibles. Saying the financial markets only include securities excludes other investments that can also maximize wealth. This conclusion is not consistent with finance as presented in this book. Thus, a financial marketplace needs to have a more comprehensive definition.

There are marketplaces for almost every good or service imaginable. Some markets are tiny and informal, and some are large and organized. Some marketplaces sell anything the sellers have available. For example, in a flea market one can buy goods ranging from food to used electronics. Some markets specialize in only certain types of products or goods. For example, the stock market sells only stocks.

Defining the financial marketplace is more difficult than it appears. It is tempting to say a financial market is a place — not necessarily a physical location; it could be virtual, as on the Internet — where buyers and sellers exchange goods and services, *typically assets*. For example in the automobile market, two assets are exchanged: the seller's car for the buyer's cash. This definition is a good start, but it's not complete when debt and equity markets are included. More on that in a minute. Thus, a financial market should include a place to exchange *all components of wealth*.

Unlike many commonly used definitions of *financial markets*, ours here will be very comprehensive.

**A financial market is a place where buyers and sellers exchange various components of wealth, which include assets, liabilities, and equity (sometimes called *net worth*).** A financial market includes various markets for exchanging everyday products and services, for example the supermarket where you can exchange cash for food. It also includes the exchange of funds between capital-market suppliers and capital-market demanders, or buyers and sellers. This capital market can include an exchange of any combination of assets, debt, and equity.

**In capital markets, suppliers and demanders meet to exchange capital for investments. Capital is money that is allocated for purchasing investments.** The return on capital, and the terms of capital structure through either debt or equity channels, should be agreed upon in the exchange. Capital-market suppliers have capital ready to be invested. However, it will only be sold if the right price (generally, in the form of interest and appreciation) is paid for the ability to use this capital. On the other hand, capital market demanders need this capital for various reasons, for example for consumption of goods or services, or to purchase an investment.

An example of a capital market is the lending or credit market, sometimes misnamed the *financing market*. An investor, a capital-market supplier, may lend his capital to a capital-market demander. The names change in this situation, and the investor is called a *creditor* and the borrower is called the *debtor*. The investor trades his cash for the investment asset, which may be a bond, and is an asset for another form of an asset. On the other hand, the capital-market demander borrows money in exchange for a promise to repay the debt with interest. In this case, the demander increases his liabilities in exchange for cash (an asset).

Another example of a capital market is the stock market. When an investor, a capital-market supplier, uses capital to buy stock shares, she trades her cash for stocks, which is an asset for another form of an asset. On the other hand, the company, the capital-market demander, sells shares of ownership for cash. In this case they trade their equity — the difference between assets and liabilities — for cash, an asset.

A final example of a capital market is the real estate market. In this market, an investor, a capital-market supplier, may use capital to buy real estate investments from a capital-market demander. Other types of capital markets include the future market, the options market, the currency market, the collectibles market, the mutual funds market, and the money market.

*Marketability* refers to how quickly a component of wealth is exchanged for another. For example, a stock listed on an organized stock exchange is said to have high marketability as opposed to a stock that is not listed on an exchange. If an investor wants to sell stock immediately, it can happen very quickly if the stock is marketable.

Some markets can be categorized as primary and secondary. In primary markets investments are offered for the first time to the public. An investment is sold only one time, for example with an initial public offering (IPO) of a stock. In a secondary market, an investment that was offered in a primary market is sold regularly to the public. For example, stocks that are traded daily on an exchange are considered part of the secondary market.

# CHAPTER 28

# Capital Overview

In the previous chapter "The Marketplace and Finance", we briefly discussed the concept of capital, but now it is time for a closer examination. Capital is one of the most important concepts in finance and economics. Yet, like many other major concepts presented in this book, its meaning is inconsistent depending on how it is used. The irony is that this term has been in use for many centuries and has been studied intensely by many economists. For example, Adam Smith discussed it thoroughly in *The Wealth of Nations*, and Karl Marx actually wrote a very large book titled *Capital*. Nevertheless, here we will attempt to clarify the term *capital* as it is used in everyday conversation and has appeared in various publications throughout the ages.

As already noted, capital is money allocated for purchasing investments. This is very different from other definitions because in this manner it is only money. From the beginning of modern economics, many economists have used the term *capital* to refer to various forms of assets. The problem is that since the science of finance has started to gain popularity, the terms used in this field are starting to converge with some of the terms of economics and accounting. Also, in the past one hundred years alone, there have been many new terms created in fields related to economics. The result is a high level of ambiguity.

In economics, *capital* generally means assets. In finance and accounting, assets describe what one owns whether it is tangible or intangible. Thus, an asset can include furniture, a stock, or intellectual property. It is time that finance and economics start to use the same vocabulary. After all, the major differences between the two subjects are a matter of whose wealth is being managed — a nation or a division of a nation versus an individual, a group, or an organization. There is no reason why simple terminology like *capital* cannot be used interchangeably between the fields, so whenever people refer to capital as an asset they can mean any form of asset as listed on the balance sheet. If the term is being used to identify only an asset then it should be called simply an asset and not capital.

*Capital assets* are sometimes referred to as a *long-term investment*. Again, why is it necessary to have two terms to say the same thing? A long term investment should just simply be called a "long term investment." Capital is also combined to form many phrases, such as *capital goods*, which refers to tangible assets that produce goods or services. This also may be translated to fit under the definition used above for investment.

Using the above definition of capital could create uniformity between economics and finance. To be clear, capital, as defined here, is money and only money. It is not clothes, furniture, or office equipment. However, it is also money that is set aside purposely for purchasing an investment. Capital is not an investment yet; it is saved money that is in a transitory state. The moment the capital is exchanged for an investment, generally in the capital marketplace, it converts into an investment.

The same is true on the opposite end of the cycle. The moment the investment is exchanged for the capital, it converts into capital (though only if it will be be reinvested). Capital can remain in transit for any duration until conversion to investment, as long as it will eventually purchase an investment.

To understand capital's relationship with savings and investments, please recall the formula used earlier in this book: savings minus investment equals savings that is not invested. We can now modify this formula to include capital: savings minus capital minus investment equals savings that is not invested or allocated to purchase investments. For example, if you save $1,000 then decide to invest $800 of it and retain the other $200 in the form of cash. This $200 is savings that is not considered invested yet. Out of that amount, let's pretend $150 will be invested once the right investment is found. This $150 would properly be labeled as capital. The remaining $50 could be labeled as pure hoarded cash.

A potential argument against the above organization of capital is that safe short-term investments may be earmarked for purchasing long-term investments and should also be labeled as capital. It is true that in common usage, investors also call this money capital. The money placed into a safe short-term investment, for example a money market mutual fund, may have all of the principle guaranteed. Due to the safety of such an investment, it may be easy to confuse it with capital when the intention is to purchase other investments. The reality is these investments must first be sold and converted to cash or its equivalent (which could be in the form of a check and not traditional cash or coin) before being reinvested into a longer-term investment. The moment it is sold, it does not retain any of the properties of an investment, and that is when it becomes true capital. This may last for seconds to hours, but short-term investments used to purchase other investments must convert to cash before converting back to investments. **To be clear, capital is not an investment yet. When it becomes an investment, it is no longer considered capital.**

Another commonly confused term is *capital gain*. Generally, this means the appreciation part of the return on an investment. This is consistent with the above definition of capital because when an investment is sold, the value in excess of the initial capital (the money invested) is the capital gain. For example, if you buy a property (your investment) for $100,000 (your initial capital) and sell it for $200,000 then your capital gain is $100,000 ($200,000 - $100,000).

Capital gains generally refer to gains made on investments that are held for more than one year (for US tax purposes). As noted above, some investments are designed for the short term, so it would be unfair for us to restrict the amount of time we can keep money in the state of capital or as an investment. *Realistically, a gain on your capital is still a capital gain whether you hold it for one day or ten years.*

Next, the term *capitalism* seems to have taken on a meaning of its own that sometimes is not in sync with other similar terms. To keep it consistent with the above definition of capital, **capitalism is an economic system where investors can freely invest capital.** This is a free market where all types of financial investors including individuals, groups, or organizations, are free to choose the destinations of their capital, investments. However, a comprehensive definition of capitalism would also include allowing financial entities to spend all of their money — and not just their capital — as they please.

To summarize, capital is a concept that has been floating around for centuries without a consistent definition. I think our definition here of capital and its related concepts has sharpened its common usage and made it more fit for practice between the sciences of finance and economics.

# CHAPTER 29

# Return and Cost of Capital

Investors don't give their money away without gaining something of value. This would be inconsistent with the definition of an investor, whose focus is to maximize wealth. Investors expect to earn returns on their capital. In the case of debt or equity exchanges, this return is the cost of capital for whoever receives the funds. That is, *return on capital* and *cost of capital* reference the same percentage (ignoring other types of fees and costs) but their meanings are different depending on what side of the table you are on. For example, if an investor is expecting to earn 5 percent on his money then that is his return on capital. Five percent is also the cost of capital for the person who is obtaining the funds.

There are various ways to calculate the cost of capital that will be studied in finance. One major method is called the weighted average cost of capital (WACC), and it accounts for the cost of all the different funding sources for an organization, for example long-term debt, preferred stock, and common stock. The various costs are all weighted and averaged together to form one complete cost of capital percentage.

Knowing your costs is essential to maximizing wealth because then you have a reference point for knowing at least how much you should make. If your costs are 10 percent, you need to make at least a 10 percent return to breakeven. If you don't think you can make back enough to cover your costs then it is generally unwise to proceed with an investment.

# CHAPTER 30

# Finance and Taxes

You may never meet your financial goals if you don't consider taxes. Wealth can only be maximized when an individual, a group, or an organization implements tax minimization strategies. Tax avoidance is necessary to accomplish a financial entity's goals, and it's a legal strategy to pay no more than one's fair share. In contrast, tax evasion is using illegal methods to reduce one's taxes.

To understand the impact of taxes, let's look at several major concepts. First, a tax deduction is different from a tax credit. A deduction results in a reduction in the taxable income for a financial entity based on its income tax rate. A tax credit will reduce the amount of taxes owed by 100 percent of the credit amount. If you have a choice between the two, take the tax credit — it will result in a higher increase in wealth.

A quick example: If you have a $1,000 tax credit then you will reduce your taxes owed by $1,000. It is analogous to receiving a check for $1,000. However, if you have a $1,000 tax deduction then your reduction will depend on your tax bracket. If it's 30 percent then your taxes will be reduced by $300 ($1,000 x 0.30). Compare this to the $1,000 reduction from the tax credit and it should be clear why the credit is more desirable.

Another aspect of taxes that must be considered is marginal rate versus average rate. The marginal rates of taxes are based on tables showing different levels of income and the amount of tax that must be paid in each. These rates vary, and generally increase as the income increases (this is called *progressive taxation*).

On the other hand, the average tax rate gives a better depiction of how much taxes one really will pay. One way to think of this rate is the actual cost of taxes, which is similar in concept to the cost of capital. Thus, a marginal rate may be 15 percent, 28 percent, etc. In early US income tax history, rates were in the ninetieth percentile. Contrarily, someone whose top tax bracket is 28 percent may have only had an average tax rate of 20 percent. This is derived by taking the total tax due and dividing it by the total taxable income. If this individual owes $10,000 in taxes, when that's divided by $50,000 in total taxable income, he will get an average tax rate of 20 percent. This is certainly less than his top marginal rate of 28 percent.

It is very important to know how to calculate before-and after-tax rates of return. This is another example of how basic math must be mastered in finance. The calculations, although very easy, must be performed without error in order to make good financial decisions. Tax-exempt bond mutual funds (and traditional bonds) are a perfect example of how before- and after-tax calculations can be helpful. Suppose you can obtain a taxable bond fund offering a 6 percent return and you are in the 28 percent income tax bracket. A risk equivalent municipal bond fund is offering a tax-free rate (for federal and state taxes) of 4 percent. Which bond is better (ignoring all other potential taxes and fees)?

There are two different ways to find out the answer, and they should not be mixed. Many students will convert both rates and make a decision instead of converting only one rate. Here, if you want to compare both rates as tax-free rates then you do not change the 4 percent. The only calculation needed is to change the 6 percent to a tax-free rate as follows: 6% x (1 – income tax rate) = 6 x 0.72 = 4.32%. Thus the taxable bond fund offers a 4.32 percent tax-free rate — which is higher than the tax-free bond fund at 4 percent. The smart choice would be the taxable bond fund.

Alternatively, you can choose to leave the taxable rate of 6 percent alone and only calculate the taxable return for the tax-free bond fund at 4 percent. This will result in two investment rates of return expressed in taxable amounts, as opposed to the first method that expressed the rates in tax-free amounts. The calculation for this method is the reverse of the first: 4% ÷ (1 – income tax rate) = 4 ÷ 0.72 = 5.56%. Thus the tax-free bond fund offers a 5.56 percent taxable rate, which is lower than the taxable-bond fund rate offered at 6 percent. The smart choice would still be the taxable bond fund.

When planning tax minimization strategies, a financial entity should be aware of the various tax laws that may impact it.

For example, there may be different deductions for individuals than for corporations. Also there are unique situations that may apply if you are a corporation, for example, the double taxation problem for corporate dividend distributions. Finally, a financial manager must be aware of the many different types of taxes that exist, including sales tax, property tax, and inheritance tax.

# CHAPTER 31

# Time Value of Money

One of the most important mathematical concepts in finance is the *time value of money*. Money has a value that generally changes for various reasons over a period of time. Financial textbooks often have conflicting definitions of the time value of money, which is sometimes referred to as TVM. A common description: the value of a unit of money (usually a dollar) is worth more today than the same unit of money in the future. This is very ambiguous, as it is not always clear if we are comparing future values to each other, present values to each other, or present values to future values, though this last case is not even sensible. Assuming though that this definition is comparing the future value of a dollar received today with the future value of a dollar received tomorrow then this definition is still not acceptable because it makes an assumption that money will always earn a positive rate of return. As discussed in the book, hoarded cash does not earn any interest. Thus, ignoring inflation and exchange rates, the value of hoarded cash is generally the same regardless of how long it exists as such.

To expand on this further, we must understand five major components of the time value of money: *time, generally expressed as N; interest rate, or I; present value of the component of wealth, or PV; payment, or PMT; and the future value of the component of wealth, or FV. All time value of money problems contain at least some of them.* Time value of money problems are concerned with the value of wealth expressed in money as it travels in a period of time — either forward to calculate the future value, or backwards to calculate the present value. The value of money cannot travel both back and forward at the same time for the same reason an automobile, plane, or boat cannot do the same. **Thus, a law of money motion is: when money is going in one direction at a specific moment, it must stay going in that direction.**

As shown with hoarded cash, money can be exactly equal to itself over time. If $1 is stashed away under the bed, in thirty years — ignoring inflation and exchange rates — it should have the same purchasing power. One dollar should still equal one dollar. However, the future value of a unit of money received today can be worth less than the value of the same unit of money received in the future. This happens directly when interest rates are negative and indirectly through inflation, which acts similarly to a negative interest rate. For example, if an individual has $1 today (PV) and invests it in a losing investment for thirty years (N) at -3 percent compound interest (I, with compound meaning it is interest earning interest), he will have only $0.40 (FV). The future value of the dollar today in this situation is clearly less than the future value of one dollar received tomorrow ($0.40 is less than $1).

If the interest rate were a positive 3 percent then the result would be the opposite. The $1 would grow in thirty years to $2.43. A dollar received today would be worth more in the future than a dollar received in the future ($2.43 is greater than $1).

What all this proves is that a better definition of the time value of money is needed. A more accurate and concise reflection of the term may be **the value of the purchasing power of money over time based on a specified interest rate.** This eliminates any ambiguity, allows for apples-to-apples comparison in terms of points in time, and accounts for any interest rate assumptions — they can be positive, zero, or negative and the definition would still hold up. Also this definition includes the inflation rate, which acts as a disguised negative interest rate. Thus, this definition allows you to calculate what your money will be worth after a necessary inflation factor is accounted for.

Time value of money problems are numerous and account for a variety of financial situations. TVM problems can include, but are not limited to calculating retirement, savings for college, and various investment values. There are four major time value of money problems: future value of a single amount, or FV (the value of a single amount in a future time period); future value of a series of deposits, or FVA (the value of an annuity or a series of payments in a future time period); present value of a single amount, or PV (the current value of a future amount based on a certain interest rate and a certain time period); and the present value of a series of deposits, or PVA (the current amount needed to make a withdrawal of a certain amount for a certain amount of time).

TVM problems can be calculated several ways: manually using the formula, with TVM tables, with a calculator, or via a computer spreadsheet. It is recommended to use more than one method to crosscheck your answers. The formula for these four major types is:

$$PV = FV \div (1+i)^n$$
$$FV = PV(1+i)^n$$
$$PVA = PMT[1 - (1+i)^{-n}] \div i$$
$$FVA = PMT[(1+i)^n - 1] \div i$$

Finally, it is important to note that there are many different financial techniques to determine if an investment is acceptable, including net present value (NPV), internal rate of return (IRR), modified internal rate of return (MIRR), and payback period. The techniques that include time value of money are usually considered the most powerful, as they consider the value of cash flows over time. It is important to use as many techniques as possible when selecting investments, but remember that no technique guarantees you'll find the perfect investment. The final selection of an investment is a human decision that should be formed through research and experience.

# CHAPTER 32

# The Agency Problem

No overview of finance would be complete without a discussion of the agency problem, which **occurs when any agents of an individual, a group, an organization, or a nation have a chance to prioritize their financial goals before the financial goals of the entity they represent.** The agents and the principal — who the agents represent — can be said to have a conflict of interest. This issue is so important because it is always present in any situation where someone is given responsibility of managing wealth for someone else, and *even the nicest people on earth have a chance of not doing the right thing in certain situations, particularly in financial situations.* The agency problem is present when a power of attorney is appointed to act on behalf of an individual. This person is granted important powers that can devastate the person he or she represents if he or she wants to. If this power of attorney signs off checks and makes decisions in order to maximize his or her wealth and not the wealth of the person he or she represents, the agency problem is underway.

One of the most popular agency problems has to do with the relationship between financial managers and corporations. There have been too many public examples — we could only guess how many are not public — where financial managers have made decisions that have maximized their own wealth while neglecting to maximize the wealth of their bosses: the stockholders who own the company. For example, a financial manager has the ability to make a company's financial statement appear like the work of a great painter. Such an illusion could pump up the financial manager's option values just at the right time for his golden parachute. Once he has retired with his millions, the company and its owners are left cleaning up the mess.

The agency problem can never be eliminated because it is human nature to maximize one's own wealth. The best solution may be to keep the problem well managed. As I've stated previously, we study finance because we want to increase our chances of survival in our modern civilization by maximizing our wealth. *It is an innate instinct for a financial manager to have the constant urge to place his or her survival needs before others'. Rare, exceptional financial managers are able to control this urge and successfully complete their assigned tasks while fulfilling their moral responsibilities to the client.*

It was no mistake that I included the word *nation* in our definition of the agency problem. Focusing on nations shifts the field of inquiry to economics. I added the term to show that economists also struggle with the agency problem. Agents who represent nations, such as politicians or economic managers, can also make decisions that maximize their own wealth while neglecting to maximize the wealth of the people of the nations they represent. Examples of this can be found throughout history. Many times it has resulted in the destruction of a nation's wealth, shortly followed by conquest by its enemies. **As in all cases, if the agency problem is not kept in check, many people can get hurt at the hands of a selfish few.**

# CHAPTER 33

# Financial Advice

Many people struggle to understand how to manage their wealth. Some refuse to learn finance for various reasons. Others may try really hard to learn finance, but without proper guidance, are led astray. This may be a result of reading the wrong books. Many financial books give either improper advice or advice that is tailored to specific people in specific circumstances. Many readers will try to follow their advice blindly and find themselves in deep water quickly.

Some people try to imitate what they learn from academic textbooks but fail to implement various strategies. One must be careful in this regard, because although many textbooks may offer good general financial information, the material is aimed at the masses. Financial advice should be specific to the individual.

Every person has different circumstances, even if it is in small degrees, which require a unique financial plan.

There are also many financial gurus who give advice via talk radio or other media channels. Just because a person is in a position to give general advice to a larger audience, it does not mean he is an expert in all financial situations — or an expert at all. This point also applies to any financial professional, for example a stock broker, a financial planner, a financial analyst. Every person who proclaims to be a financial professional should not be trusted blindly. Find out about their academic and practical track records before you put your trust in so-called experts.

You may want to ask: What degrees in finance have they achieved? Higher degrees are preferable because they demonstrate the experts have put time into learning about the concepts of their science.

Also, what kind of publications have they completed? What certifications, designations, or licenses do they have? You may want to make sure each one they list is valid. Also, how many years of experience do they have in their field? A financial professional with plenty of education but limited experience may not have acquired enough understanding of the practical complexities of their specialty. Finally, are they successful investors? True credibility can be established in finance by those who practice what they preach.

It is more sensible to work with professionals who not only talk the talk but have walked the walk. This makes sense in any other area of life, and it should certainly make sense when dealing with your money. For example, it may be a dangerous affair to eat at a restaurant where you know that the chef has never sampled her own food. You would also be taking a chance by going to a hairdresser who has never successfully cut his own hair, or a doctor who has never treated himself. If a financial professional cannot manage his own wealth properly, it may be a catastrophic assumption that he is capable of managing the wealth of someone else.

I wrote this chapter as a caution, particularly for those with little or no financial experience. Unfortunately, in my experience in the field, I have seen too many innocent people fallen victim to financial professionals who have been incompetent, reckless, indifferent, or all of the above. Some cases amounted to tragedies of only a few hundred dollars; others were lost life savings.

*The result of implementing bad financial advice can be devastating.* If financial advice is needed, the best approach is to be cautious about whom you trust. Do your homework on the financial professional, and get a second opinion if possible. As you become more financially savvy, it becomes easier to sort through good and bad financial advice before making a decision. **Ultimately, every student of finance should become the master of his or her financial destiny and make all of his or her own major financial decisions.** Also, if a financial professional is needed, it is important always to be a part of the decision-making process. After all, who cares more about your money than you?

# CHAPTER 34

# Finance and Health

There is a high correlation between finance and health. Generally, the more wealth an individual has, the higher the odds are of a comfortable existence. As I've mentioned, learning finance is a necessity for survival in modern civilization. If an individual does not know how to manage his wealth then he may dance at or below the poverty line his whole life. Currently in America health insurance is one of the highest expenses an individual has to pay if his employer does not offer this benefit. It has become so high that many Americans choose not to have insurance; rather they take their chances. It's not that they don't want insurance, but it's too expensive.

On the contrary, the cost of insurance results in many other Americans being insurance rich and cash poor. This makes it extremely difficult for many people to maximize their wealth, especially when the costs are inflating astronomically every year.

This American health crisis results in a situation where the wealthier you are, the higher the chances you have of accessing better health-care options. *To be more concise, under the current American healthcare system, the wealthier you are the healthier you could be.* For example, consider a wealthy person with a net worth of $5 million to $10 million. For this person obtaining continuous health insurance should not be too much of a strain on the monthly budget. The best medical coverage will be available for this individual and his family whenever it is necessary. The family will be covered for annual checkups and major surgeries, all of which may result in longer lives for these individuals.

If these same people did not have health insurance and a medical emergency occurred, they would be forced to deal with the problem without being hospitalized. This may certainly result in a shorter life, especially if there is an urgent need for modern medical treatment that they cannot afford.

A true student of finance strives to learn about better ways to manage her wealth in order to live a more comfortable and healthier existence. If she can maximize her wealth then she will improve her odds of obtaining necessary medical treatment when needed. People still can live comfortably without paying for medical insurance if they don't ever need major treatment. Many would rather treat themselves than go to a doctor. This may or may not work, but the risk still exists. If a serious emergency happens that requires access to modern medical facilities, for example something that requires immediate brain or heart surgery, these people may not receive the proper treatment.

This positive correlation between wealth and health is not true in all countries. Some have universal health coverage where every citizen gets access to the same or at least high-quality medical treatment whenever needed. It appears that in these situations, the goal of maximizing wealth has little or no effect on increasing the odds of being healthier from the standpoint of quality health-care access.

The positive correlation between wealth and health was not always true in America. Before modern medicine started to advance rapidly in the late nineteenth century, most wealthy individuals had access to the best doctors. However, it did little good for them as the best doctors in those days barely knew the benefits of sterilization. The medical community of the past did not have the advanced knowledge of health that exists today. The result was that the wealthier you were, the less healthy you would be if you opted for the current medical treatments of those days (including bloodletting and surgery with unsterilized tools).

Understanding finance is also important for your health because the better you are able to gain control over your wealth, the lower your stress levels may be. Stress from worrying about wealth can manifest internally and cause serious health problems. *Financial stress* is a serious issue and may come from losing a job, a reduction in income, market values of assets dropping significantly, owing too much debt, and many other similar issues. This is not implying that wealthy people don't experience stress. However, the degrees of stress may be much smaller for a wealthier person with successful control over his wealth than for another individual of similar age who is struggling daily to pay his bills. This stress can increase exponentially if one also is responsible for the welfare of a family.

In general, higher levels of wealth provide an individual with a better path to higher levels of health. A wealthy individual may have better access to quality medical treatment as well as reduced levels of financial stress. This, of course, assumes that one chooses to take advantage of these options and uses the knowledge learned from finance to maintain these options.

# CHAPTER 35

# Finance and Ethics

At this point you may be wondering what role ethics has in the science of finance. Ethics is the moral principles that guide an individual, a group, an organization, or a nation (in the case of economics) in their decision-making processes. Considering this book's definition, purpose, and goals for both finance and economics, it is easy to presume that these sciences, with the focus on wealth maximization, can only lead human civilization to the path of destruction. However, let's consider the whole case to dismiss this fallacy.

To understand the ethical argument, first let's recall the significance of managing wealth — the root of the sciences of finance and economics. The argument can boil down to two major options: to eliminate wealth or recognize the importance of it, and continue down the path of wealth accumulation. If we eliminate wealth, whether partially or fully, then humans may regress as a collective whole. The strategy is an old idea from the days of socialism in the early nineteenth century, and then refined by Karl Marx with his original ideas for communism. The idea sounded great in print, but in reality it diverted the attention of human progress for more than one hundred years. In the end it proved useless, as demonstrated by the Soviet Union's collapse in the 1980s.

Besides, at this point, think of what would happen if we were to eliminate all forms of wealth. There would be no money. Without it we could not perform even simple transactions effectively, like buying groceries. Then again, there may not be any more grocery stores because there would be little incentive to open one. There would be no businesses without wealth, and our system, at best, would digress to the days of inefficient bartering. This brings us to a major point of this book: **understanding finance is not an option; it is a necessity.**

By now it should be clear that everyone needs wealth for various reasons. Thus, many may wonder if the goal of maximizing wealth can be harmful to humans. It is important to consider that in a capitalistic free market, entities have the option to consume and invest at their own free will. From a moral perspective, money is not evil or good. It is a symbol of stored wealth and a tool to exchange goods and services. Money itself, whether in the form of gold or paper, does not have a human conscience to decipher right from wrong. **It is the person, group, organization, or nation that controls the money that has the ability to perform acts of evil or good by choosing to consume**

**unethical products or services, donate to unethical causes, or pursue unethical investments.**

Eliminating the current system of wealth may do little but regress civilization, as it will take away the tools for conducting the proper, necessary business that links humans together. The real problem is to ensure that the people who have money are doing the right things to promote the common good for all people. This system can work best in a completely free market with a government run truly by the people.

There are many examples, in corporate America alone within the past fifty years, of unethical practices by management. These events give the field of finance a bad name because they divert public attention to focus only on the bad side of the science. *First, it is certainly wrong to implement unethical financial activities on other humans, especially in the case of corporate managers who neglect their responsibilities to put their wealth before the owners they represent (please see the chapter titled "The Agency Problem"). Second, it is certainly wrong to implement unethical financial activities that will do harm to society as a whole. Finally, it is certainly wrong to implement unethical financial activities that will do harm to the well-being of our planet and all of its living inhabitants.*

There are also many examples of the good that money and wealth can do. Of course what is *good* can be very subjective. However, most people would agree that charities and philanthropists who donate money to, for example, curing diseases and protecting the environment, are generally considered ethical distributors of wealth. There are many examples where donated wealth has saved or improved people's lives. These charities and philanthropists choose to use their wealth to help society in some specific, positive way.

Finally, ethical decisions, contrary to popular belief, actually result in long-term profits for a business. Those that take a chance and perform unethical actions may not be around for the long term to make any more money. Once a business loses the trust of its customers, its wealth will slowly deplete. On the other hand, a business that promotes ethical behavior gains the long-term trust of its customers, so it will survive and be profitable in the long term (assuming its owners are also successful at managing their wealth).

To conclude, the components of wealth and the goals of finance are not obstacles to promoting good life on our planet. The obstacle to overcome is ensuring there is a healthy financial system in place to promote better ways to improve the quality of life for everyone. There will always be a few bad apples in a bunch. This is part of life and should not be a deterrent. The challenge is to ensure more successful, wealthy financial managers with good intentions are included amongst our great leaders. Wealthy people control many of the major decisions of the world. *Wealthy financial managers are a valuable asset to a financial entity and a nation if they know how to employ their wealth to have a positive impact on the greatest number of people and our planet.* The ethical challenge of finance is to find better ways to help people manage their wealth while also considering the ethical impact of their decisions.

The ethical challenge of economics is to ensure that a nation's wealthy people are using their wealth wisely in the best interest of the people of the nation. This is not to advocate government control over anyone's wealth. Instead economists should strive to ensure a competitive environment where the most successful, ethical financial managers rise to the top. This could help to create optimal ethical financial and economic environments.

# CHAPTER 36

# Finance and the Environment

It is important to include ethical consequences in the financial decision-making process. Individuals, groups, organizations, and nations should maximize wealth while simultaneously striving to eliminate any negative consequences it may have to other humans. In addition, they should strive to eliminate any negative consequences for other species and the health of our planet.

In earlier civilizations, the consequences of wealth management were not as severe as they are now. Humans are currently capable of utilizing wealth to destroy everything on earth if a consensus is formed and agreed upon. It is no longer a question of "can we destroy our planet?" but "do we want to destroy it?" With such great powers entrusted to us, humans have a responsibility to take care of all the various forms of nature that share our world.

At some point, hopefully before the damage is irreversible, humans should collectively agree to maximize the quality of all components of our environment by investing in a healthier planet. **Environmental goals can only be accomplished when more wealth is directed toward them.** This can only happen when spending money on environmental protection by all entities is made a priority. Some examples of positive environmental impacts that can be caused by wealth distribution include cleaning up air, land, and water pollution and avoiding unnecessary waste of precious resources.

This is why finance is a necessity. Learning how to manage wealth is not only important for the survival of individuals, groups, and organizations but for the environment for which we are responsible. What good is maximizing wealth if we do not have a quality environment to enjoy it in? Ensuring our wealth is funneled toward things that are good rather than bad for our environment must be an absolute priority for current civilization and the generations that will supersede us.

# CHAPTER 37

# International Finance

Managing wealth successfully can consist of many complex decisions that need to be made. It is even more complex when managing wealth for an individual, a group, or an organization that has wealth spread over various countries. International finance is a specialty of finance that pertains to managing domestic and foreign wealth for an individual, a group, or an organization. This field of finance can be as simple as an individual investor purchasing some stock in a foreign stock exchange or as complicated as conducting everyday business for large, multinational corporations.

In general, the concepts of finance in the foreign setting are the same as they are at home. Yet there are several other elements that can make international finance tricky. For example, if one is conducting business in another country she will need to study all aspects of the country and its people. An investor or business entity will need to know the economic data of a country, including population size, average income, and demographics. They will also need to research the culture to see if the product or service they will offer is acceptable by their target market. For example, it may be unwise to sell beef in a country where religion does not allow people to eat it. Not only may this activity be unprofitable but it also may be highly insulting to the people of that country.

Investors or business entities should also study the currency market of each country in which they plan on doing business. Exchange-rate fluctuations can ruin wealth for a financial entity if the entity does not plan correctly. For those that want to conduct international business but do not want the currency risk associated with it, there are hedging strategies available. For example, by utilizing tools such as various currency derivatives, the only worry may be the simple cost of the transaction.

Also, financial entities should know the political stability of the country they wish to enter. If the country is unstable, the local government may decide one day to possess all of the wealth of the foreign individuals, groups, or organizations in their country. This activity is called *expropriation*, and it creates a substantial risk for businesses and investors. Imagine a company that spent millions of dollars and many years building a business with thousands of employees in another country. Then one day the government decided to make this business state-owned. This would be extremely devastating for the company and its owners. This would also deter any future businesses from opening up in that country. Thus, even though expropriation may not be an intelligent strategy on behalf of the foreign nation in the long run, the possibility always exists. Many nations throughout history have done many economically foolish acts, and it certainly may happen again.

Finally, international financial managers should work with a group of international attorneys because the laws of each country can be obstacles to conducting business. Knowing the laws of the foreign countries where wealth will be allocated will only make the process smoother and help to minimize the international legal risk. It is also important to know the tax laws of the foreign country, so a foreign accountant may need to be involved as well.

These are some of the many unique issues that international financial managers will need to be aware of. However, the fundamentals of finance are generally the same. For example, multinational corporations still use financial statements and refer back to many of the same financial theories taught in academia. In addition, many common investment techniques for finding domestic investments are still used to find international investments, for example net present value and the profitability index. Diversification is still an essential financial technique. Actually, in many cases, international diversification may be the main reason why financial managers decide to manage wealth abroad.

As stated earlier, the management of wealth in order to meet the goal of continuously maximizing wealth becomes a condition for survival. As the world becomes more globalized, international finance is becoming more relevant. Individuals, groups, and organizations must continue to find better ways to maximize their wealth in order to survive despite increasing international competition. If it is difficult to increase wealth under normal domestic conditions, it becomes even more difficult when competing with financial entities of other countries, especially if their labor is cheaper.

When other nations are considered, new populations of competition emerge. This is a major issue that economists encounter at the national level. Should nations close their doors to business with foreign nations to avoid unnecessary competition, or should they embrace it? History has taught us that neglecting free trade, although it may be beneficial for certain businesses, generally results in the lesser good for all mankind. Thus, an open-door free-trade system between countries is generally the best option for nations and financial entities in the long run, despite the unique challenges it creates.

# CHAPTER 38

# Financial Occupations

Finance is a subject that is relevant to all individuals regardless of their occupations. It doesn't matter if a person is in retail or wholesale, the service industry or the product industry, or if he works with liquid or illiquid products. Money, and prices of goods and services expressed in money terms, truly is the glue that holds all businesses together. People need to know how to manage money and other parts of wealth in all stages of their life cycle. People may have many jobs in the courses of their lives but the knowledge gained from finance is portable to all of them.

Even though finance is necessary for all occupations, there are jobs that are specifically created to deal with the various forms of wealth management. First, there are various positions in the banking field. One can start as a bank teller who handles customers' deposits and withdrawals. This is generally an entry level job that can help one get their foot in the door. Eventually a teller can become a branch manager or supervisor who is responsible for managing the wealth of a particular bank branch. He may have to report to many more bosses, for example, regional managers (depending on how big the bank is). There may also be loan specialists whose role is to build a book of clients to lend money to. The bank underwriter may have to approve these loans before the process can continue. Some other banking jobs include wealth managers for clients, investment specialists, and even stock brokers. Finally, there are executive bank roles including the president and vice president.

An individual can also become a financial planner (sometimes called a *financial consultant* or *financial advisor*). These are really financial managers when their role is very comprehensive. However, if clients want them to perform only specific acts such as buying investments, and refuses to disclose optional information about themselves, this limits the amount of service that can be expected of these professionals. Please review the chapter "The Necessity of Financial Planning" for more information about financial planners.

Financial analysts are also very prominent in the financial profession. Their main function is to review underlying securities to make recommendations for acceptance. Becoming a financial analyst requires a significant amount of training and examinations to ensure competency.

There are also annuity and insurance salespeople. There are regular annuities and variable annuities; selling the latter may require additional licensing and training, as there is an added stock component. There are also many different types of insurance agents. Some are licensed to sell all types of insurance while others focus on a specific type. For example, a comprehensive independent insurance salesperson may sell every insurance product available, from medical to life. On the other hand, some insurance salespeople only sell one type of insurance for one company, for example, car insurance from Company XYZ.

If one includes marketing in the science of finance then there are a wide range of jobs for that as well, ranging from telemarketing to marketing directors.

A final example of a financial occupation is an investor. This job may take on different forms depending on whether one is the investor or the agent of an investor. Financial managers of mutual funds are agents of the many investors of the fund. Their job is to maximize the wealth of their clients, and they are compensated for their service. A stock broker is another job where one can act as an agent of an investor. Stock-brokers generally recommend stock investments.

Another financial job requires saved capital before one is hired. A person can become an investor, whether part time or full time, if he can employ his own capital to maximize his wealth. *Ideally, all students of finance should strive to become successful investors, as this can accelerate their journey to financial independence.*

The above occupations in the field of finance are just a sample of the many that exist. Many more jobs will be created too as the financial industry continues to develop.

# CHAPTER 39

# The Future of Finance

This book may have a significant impact on how finance, economics, and many related fields are viewed. If its message reaches the right places, I conjecture, there may be a major restructuring of how finance is taught. This would be a positive outcome and would allow finance to reach the level of respect it deserves.

There may be a day when Nobel Prizes are awarded in the field of finance. This event would demonstrate that finance is finally distinguished as an internationally recognized, unique science. For financialists this would be an historical, celebrated milestone. However, for this event to occur, it is very important that the existing pioneers in modern finance and other leaders in financial academia and in practice unite. They must agree on the fundamentals of finance and its purpose as a science.

If this book does not have the intended effect then a different outcome may occur. Finance, economics, and related subjects may continue down the path of obscurity. More subjects may be created and taught at the university level without a clear connection to the bigger picture. Academia may end up with plenty of business, finance, and economics courses that overlap each other. The final result may be one big, unorganized mess that has passed the tipping point of no return.

Regardless of whether or not my recommendations are implemented, finance still contains the risk, like all other major sciences, of its scientists misdirecting their efforts onto an evil path of destruction. Considering the gravity of the focus of finance, the consequences of this situation are more severe than in many other sciences. Currently there are many "scholars" in finance and economics who are focused on creating more-complex financial instruments that are unlikely to benefit society. At this point the only thing these scholars should be creating is a reorganization of finance and economics.

Finance and economics need to regroup and do some soul searching before they are in proper form to create any more financial instruments, if any are necessary. Considering that the past fifty years have seen a record number of financial innovations, it may be wise to spend some time revisiting their purposes and ensuring these creations are actually productive. If financial innovations do more harm than good to society then they need to be revised or eliminated. **Financial products should be designed to help make society function better, not worse.**

# CHAPTER 40

# Conclusions

Finance is a beautiful science that is separate and distinct from all sciences the world has ever produced. In this book, the significance of the science of finance was demonstrated and many of its concepts were revisited. The most essential revisited concepts were a restatement of its definition, purpose, and major goal. First, finance was defined as the science of management of wealth for an individual, a group, or an organization. Second, the purpose of finance was stated: to continuously seek, analyze, and implement better ways to maximize wealth for an individual, a group, or an organization. Third, the major goal of finance was stated: to continuously maximize wealth for an individual, a group, or an organization. The definition, purpose, and major goal of finance are clearly different from those of economics.

Although both of these subjects focus on wealth maximization, economics pertains to a nation or a division of a nation. In other words, economics is not finance, and finance is not economics.

Finance as a science has been half asleep for most of history. Recently it was awakened by changes in human civilization. For the first time in history, wealth management has become so important to the majority of a nation's population instead of a wealthy few. This may be the result of more freedom for the common people, technological advances, and economic policies. Whatever the reason, the time for finance to be recognized as a powerful and productive science is now.

Finance is an exciting science that deals with survival. If one cannot manage his wealth properly then he may find himself struggling in many aspects throughout his life. This does not imply that wealthy people do not struggle. However, a wealthy individual generally has better options to increase his probability of successfully surviving and eliminating the financial stress associated with being poor.

This book also introduced the term *financialist* to describe the financial scientist. Many other terms have been reviewed from a different perspective as well, including investor, speculator, gambler, financial manager, financial planner, financier, wealth, investment, savings, various markets, capital, return, risk, agency problem, business, time value of money, and ethics.

Many randomly placed business and finance subjects were better organized under two major categories: personal finance and group and organizational finance. There was also a radical inclusion of certain miscellaneous subjects under the umbrella science of finance. That is, subjects like human resources, accounting, marketing, and business were always thought to be related to finance. However, with closer examination, it was demonstrated that they are actually subsciences of finance because their ultimate goal is wealth maximization. All of these subjects help complete the puzzle of learning better ways to manage wealth for individuals, groups, and organizations.

The subject of financial economics was also given a place, but in the context of managing the wealth of a nation or the wealth of a division of a nation. On the other hand, a new field was created called economic finance, which allows for understanding economic concerns in the context of managing wealth for financial entities. These subjects are another example of how finance and economics are highly related yet may be very different depending on who the focus of wealth maximization is. Different issues can affect maximizing wealth for economic entities versus financial entities. This is a major reason why these sciences need to be explored separately.

There is an old saying that throughout history has seldom been proven false: "necessity is the mother of invention". At the time of this writing, human civilization has reached one of its highest points of wealth in history. There are more millionaires than the world has ever known. Despite this, America still has a significant poverty problem. Furthermore, the world is exponentially accelerating towards complete globalization, and extreme poverty still exists throughout the majority of the planet. Economics has tried to resolve these problems alone, but had mixed success, possibly because it has been looking at the problem only from one perspective. If the focus is shifted and the problem is viewed from the perspective of all parties including individuals, groups, and organizations, then better solutions may be visible.

Economics is not finance, but the two sciences united may be able to better resolve some of the world's biggest problems. The first step in making this happen is proper classification and distinction of the two fields. Our society can no longer afford to ignore the truth. Finance, although always present informally, has been formally designed recently for the reason of necessity.

Now more than ever, there is a necessity to recognize the significance of finance. Now more than ever, there is a necessity to learn the science of finance.

# Index

Business law, 89
Business: defined, 101
Businessman, 106
Businessperson, 106
Businesswoman, 106

Capital gain, 160
Capital market: defined,
    154-155
Capital: defined, 154,
    158-159
Capitalism, 73; defined, 161
CAPM theory, 7, 41, 119-120
Cash flow statement, 115-117
Certificate of deposits (CDs),
    145-151
Coin: history of, 34-35
Collectibles, 145-151
Communism, 72-73, 81, 186
Corporate finance, 7, 95-96
Cost of capital, 163-164;
    WACC, 164
Credit market, 155
Current ratio, 117, 125

Debt: history of, 35-37
Democracies, 71
Democratic republics, 71
Department of Revenue, 66

Derivatives, 37, 43, 150, 153,
    194
Dictatorships, 71
Disability insurance, 93
Diversification: defined,
    143-144
Division of labor, 2, 26
Domestication, 32

Earnings per share, 117-118
East India Companies, 36
Economic entities, 65
Economic finance, 86, 95, 205
Economic financialist, 87
Economics: defined, 14-15,
    63; primary goal, 68;
    purpose, 67; secondary
    goals, 68-69
Education planning, 91-92
Efficient frontier, 120
Efficient market hypothesis
    (EMH), 42, 121, 144
Einstein, Albert, 3
Entrepreneurial finance, 95, 98
Estate planning, 91, 94
Ethics: defined, 185
Expropriation, 194

Fama, Eugene, 42, 121

Internal rate of return (IRR), 172
Investing, 97-98; defined, 128
Investment: defined, 128
Investor: defined, 133

Keynes, John Maynard, 5-6
Keynesian, 72-74

Laissez faire, 72-73
Liquidity: defined, 13, 146
Long-term care insurance, 91
Lynch, Peter, 121

M & M propositions, 7
Management, 95-97; defined, 10, 63
Managerial finance, 89, 95-96
Marginal tax rate, 166
Marketability: defined, 156
Marketing, 97-100
Markowitz, Harry, 7, 41-44, 86, 119-120
Marx, Karl, 73, 186; (*Capital*), 157
MBA, 57, 107
Medici family, 36
Merton, Robert, 7, 42-43
Mesopotamia, 99
Miller, Merton, 7, 41-43, 119-120

Modified internal rate of return (MIRR), 172
Modigliani, Franco, 7, 41-43, 119-120
Monarchies, 71-72
Monetarism, 72-73
Money markets, 131-133, 145-146
Money, 29; defined, 10-11
Mutual funds, 145-151

Negative correlation, 144
Net present value (NPV), 172
Nobel Prize, 7-8, 43-44, 201
Nonprofit financial management, 95
Nonprofit organization, 103-104; defined, 103

Opportunity cost, 46

Payback period, 172
PE ratio, 117-118
Personal finance: defined, 90; primary goal, 91; purpose, 91
Philadelphia, 36-37, 65
Philanthropists, 19, 187-188
Planning for parenthood, 91-92
Progressive taxation, 166
Public finance, 89, 95-96